BLAUW'S
VEGGIE KITCHEN

BLAUW'S VEGGIE KITCHEN

Restaurant Blauw's Crew Presents
70 Authentic Vegetarian and Vegan Recipes

TERRA

TABLE OF CONTENTS

TABLE OF CONTENTS

Preface — 10
Introduction — 14
Indonesian Culinary Culture — 16
Common Ingredients — 18
Cooking Techniques + Tips & Tricks — 26
How to Create a Vegetarian
   or Vegan Rice Table — 30

THE TEAM AT RESTAURANT BLAUW

Hendra Subandrio — 36
Yunita Dirmayanti — 38
Uma Phetkaw — 40
Donni Setiawan Suganda — 42
Mulfi Yasir — 44
Felix Pontoh — 46
Michel E Saleh — 48
Dewi Peters — 50
Vera Atika — 52
Peter de Groot — 54
Tirta Sulamit — 56

SOUPS

Sayur Asem — 62
Sop Jamur — 64
Sop Labu — 66
Sop Tahu Santan — 68

MAIN COURSES

Asem Pade Nangka Muda — 72
Bami Timun Jepang — 74
Bihun Goreng Kampung — 76
Bubur Manado / Tinutuan — 78
Cager Telur Madura — 80
Sop Sayur Santan — 82
Gulai Boerenkool — 84
Jamur Masak Wijen — 86
Kwetieuw Sayur — 88
Lodeh Tempe Pete — 90
Nangka Rica Rica — 92
Opor Tahu Tempe — 94
Oseng Tempe — 96
Pepes Tahu Betawi — 98
Rendang Nangka Muda — 100
Sambal Goreng Tahu Kentang — 102
Sayur Daun Singkong — 104
Sayur Kubis — 106
T3 Bumbu Bali — 108
Tahu Acar — 110
Tahu Goreng Asam Manis — 112
Tahu Tempe Tauco — 114
Telur Semur — 116
Tempe Sambal Matah — 118
Terong Bakar Pecak Pati — 120
Terong Kecap — 122
Terong Madu — 124
Tofu Sambal Tauco — 126
Tumis Kangkung Bawang Putih — 128

STREET FOOD

Jamur Bungkus Karee	132
Kroket Lodeh	134
Lumpia Tahu	136
Pepesan Jamur	138
Perkedel Jagung	140
Perkedel Tahu Donni	142
Sate Jamur	144

SIDE DISHES

Acar Campur	148
Acar Ketimun	150
Acar Nanas	152
Gohu	154
Gulai Nangka	156
Nasi Goreng	158
Pare Pare Jawir	160
Perkedel Tahu Yunita	162
Sambal Goreng Buncis	164
Sambal Tempe	166
Saus Kacang	168
Sayur Acar Kuning	170
Quick Nasi Kuning	172
Telor Kuning	174
Tumis Bayam	176
Tumis Jamur Kemangi	178
Tumis Kangkung	180

SALADS

Asinan Jakarta	184
Mie Terong Dan Salad Mangga	186
Pecel	188
Salad Mie Jamur	190
Salad Tahu Jamur	192

SWEETS AND DESSERTS

Barongko	196
Bubur Kacang Hijau	198
Bubur Ketan Hitam	200
Es Cendol	202
Kue Ubi Manis	204
Puding Santan Pandan	206
Tape Ketan Hitam with Vanilla Ice Cream	208
Wingko Babat	210

Acknowledgments	214
Index	218
Credits	224

PREFACE

In Indonesia, dining with our families is an important and cherished tradition. For me, Indonesian cuisine is synonymous with the comfort and warmth that I find with my family. I strive to convey this feeling to our guests when they dine with us, making them feel welcome and part of our extended family.

This distinctive "Blauw feeling" is the guiding principle for our entire approach to our guests and our team. Naturally, our passion for delicious cuisine, quality ingredients, and hospitality is paramount for me and my team. The acknowledgment of our efforts by Michelin, which awarded us the 2022 Bib Gourmand, has certainly reinforced our dedication to our values.

My deep love and passion for Indonesian cuisine was cultivated from an early age. My father spent part of his youth in the former Dutch East Indies (now Indonesia) before coming to the Netherlands at the age of thirteen. At home we frequently cooked Indonesian dishes. As a child, I would help my father to prepare the *rijsttafel* ("rice table"), a feast of many small dishes reserved for special occasions.

I come from a hardworking, entrepreneurial family, and when I entered the hospitality industry at the age of seventeen I joined their ranks. My journey took me through many areas of this sector, including luxury dining and Michelin-starred restaurants, which reinforced my deep respect for top-notch service and exceptional food. When as a consultant I had the opportunity to take over Restaurant Blauw Amsterdam-Utrecht, I strove to create a relaxed, informal atmosphere while still holding onto these values. That was in 2013, and I believe we have achieved this admirably.

Earlier, we used to take a photo at each table, just as we would at family gatherings. These pictures were compiled into an album on our website. Times have evolved, and now that everyone has a camera on their phone, we have discontinued this practice. However, we still often help guests capture memorable moments at Blauw with their own phone.

Both of our restaurants boast a fantastic team of employees who are dedicated to our goals. We work essentially as a family. After some challenging years and a few departures, I am pleased with the steadfast core team that remains.

When you step into Blauw, whether in Utrecht or Amsterdam, your attention is immediately drawn to a large family photograph that adorns the wall. This photograph holds special significance, and dates back over 120 years. It captures the value we place in family, and the warmth and nurturing that family can provide. In Indonesia, family is very important, and serves as the nucleus around which life revolves. At Blauw, you can see the essence of family beyond its customary meaning: people who enjoy making others happy and comfortable by preparing and serving delicious, heartwarming food. As I said, the idea of family runs deep within our team. To express the sense of belonging we feel as the "Blauw family," it felt natural to create a cookbook together. Each member of our team contributed their favorite recipes, which often have a special personal meaning for them. *Blauw's Veggie Kitchen* is the story of our employees, who carry within them a treasury of beautiful dishes, cherished both in their memories and in their hearts. Cooking is an art born of the heart, an expression of love, affection, and comfort. Our hope is to convey this sentiment within our restaurants and through the pages of this book.

Henk van Hees,
Owner of Restaurant Blauw Amsterdam-Utrecht

INTRODUCTION

Contrary to expectations, the house style and interiors of Blauw's restaurants make use of lots of red. The name Blauw—which means blue in Dutch—does not, in fact, refer to the color but to "de blauw hap" ("the blue bite"): nasi goreng, or fried rice. This meal was traditionally served on Wednesdays to Dutch-East Indian naval staff, also known as the "blauwe jongens" ("blue boys").

At Blauw, we serve authentic Indonesian dishes, drawing inspiration from the entire Indonesian archipelago. By authentic we mean pure Indonesian cuisine, which has not been influenced by Dutch tastes. This is distinct from Indo food, which is a fusion of European and Indonesian flavors characterized by culinary improvisation. In Indo cuisine, if ingredients were unavailable, other options were substituted. This has led to distinct dishes for each tradition: for instance, kale with sambal is Indo, while cucumber with peanut sauce is Indonesian.

From a historical, sociological, emotional, and cultural perspective, the differences between Indo and Indonesian cuisines run much deeper. Indeed, the distinctions between Indo and Indonesian culinary traditions are too complex to be encapsulated in a single sentence.

Indonesia is made up of over 16,000 islands, with each community boasting its own rich and diverse culinary culture. Food is a crucial aspect of Indonesian culture; it is a vital link among people, and is closely tied to family and a sense of belonging. In Indonesia, the work culture is inseparable from family dynamics. Eating, sleeping, working, and communicating happen seamlessly, and is one of life's significant goals. As a result, there are many thriving small family businesses, with each family member contributing.

At Blauw, we approach cooking with respect. We want to create an environment where everyone feels welcome and at home, irrespective of their religion, origin, or dietary preferences. In both restaurants, a family photograph adorns one of the walls. The photo is approximately 120 years old, and the girl standing in the lower right-hand corner is the grandmother of Blauw's founder. In this unusual photograph, people with different skin colors form a close-knit group, and everyone belongs to one family.

Sustainable food culture is a high priority for us, and so we offer a wide array of vegetarian and vegan dishes. With vegetables, tofu (tahu), and tempeh (tempe) as integral parts of traditional Indonesian cuisine, there are numerous vegetarian and vegan options. At Blauw, we like finding ways to combine sustainability and tradition. Indonesian food captures the essence of dining with family, providing a sense of homecoming. It is the ultimate compliment to hear guests say, during or after meals, "It's almost as delicious as my grandmother's." We hope the recipes in this book enable you to elicit such sentiments from those you welcome to your table at home.

INDONESIAN CULINARY CULTURE

Indonesian cuisine is rich and diverse. This is not surprising, considering that Indonesia is made up of over 16,000 islands. Geography, climate, and religion all play a significant role in determining the dishes served. Although Indonesia is predominantly Islamic—it is the largest Islamic country in the world—about ten percent of the population is Christian, and in Bali, Hinduism is widely practiced.

Because of Hindu influences, pork is consumed in Bali but in Java it is not. While pigs are raised in Java, they are less prevalent in the street scene. Chinese immigrants who settled in Indonesia have access to pork. However, for the majority of Indonesia's Islamic population, pork is not a part of the menu. The province of Aceh on the island of Sumatra maintains the most traditional approach. Although there are numerous cultural and political sensitivities, Indonesians tend to avoid discussing these issues, a characteristic often observed in Asian culture: conflict avoidance. This trait is mirrored in their culinary culture, which is incredibly diverse.

It would be inaccurate to claim that Indonesian cuisine is exclusively spicy, because the spiciness varies across regions. Due to the influence of Indian cuisine, West Sumatra features many curry-like dishes and tends to be spicy. Javanese dishes are milder and sweeter, particularly in Central Java. North Sulawesi (also called Noord-Celebes in the Netherlands) is known for its seafood, with dishes that are brightly flavored, well-seasoned, and spicy. Bali is known for dishes that make abundant use of vegetables and pork.

The Dutch who lived in Indonesia before the revolution were located primarily in Jakarta, Java. This is why the Dutch are familiar with less spicy cuisine. The use of sambal (a spicy condiment) alongside meals is typically Dutch. In Indonesia, sambal is added to food during preparation as a flavoring. Since this resulted in meals that were too spicy for many Dutch people, sambal began to be served on the side.

Whether people consume primarily plant-based food depends on the region they live in. In Bandung, for

instance, vegetables are a staple due to the city's geographical features: lush greenery, fertile soil, and a climate suitable for growing vegetables. Java utilizes over fifty percent of its land for rice paddies (sawahs). Generally, rice is grown in the valleys and on the plains. Meat consumption in Indonesia depends largely on one's financial means. Some people eat only rice with sambal, while others add vegetables and maybe eggs. Those with higher incomes include meat, fish, or poultry in their daily meals. Geography also determines the menu: coastal towns favor fish, while inland areas focus on meat and poultry. Because there is a risk of spoilage when transporting harvested fish in a warm climate, fish are transported alive and slaughtered at the destination. The beloved dish known as rendang—beef stewed in spicy coconut sauce—can have a dry or wetter form, based on the region. Surveys show that rendang and nasi goreng (fried rice) are the most widely consumed Indonesian dishes worldwide. Rendang is to Indonesia as split pea soup is to the Netherlands. Each recipe in Indonesian cuisine has a unique preparation method, and each chef adds their own special twist. A recipe is a guideline. Suppose that the recipe calls for ten peppers, but one pepper is hotter than the others. During preparation, cooks will smell and taste a dish to see whether there should be more or less of a certain flavor, and then make adjustments according to taste. Introducing variations to a recipe, personally interpreting and tailoring a dish, is how diversity in culinary cultures is born. The same principle applies to the presentation of dishes. In this book we sometimes recommend adding garnishes, like an edible flower or a few lemongrass rings, to make a dish more visually appealing. Of course, these garnishes are optional and do not determine the taste. Have fun, and unleash your creativity when presenting your dishes!

INDONESIAN CULINARY CULTURE

COMMON INGREDIENTS

Many of the savory recipes in this book start with "Finely dice an onion and finely chop a clove of garlic." Onions, shallots, and garlic form the basis of a dish. Chili paste (sambal), peppers, fresh herbs, and spices are also used in most dishes. Often, these are first ground into a "bumbu," which is a spice blend or paste. To do this, it's best to use a food processor or blender. If you chop the ingredients finely, you can also easily measure and puree them with a hand blender. Traditionally, a mortar and pestle is used to make a bumbu. This process is different from using a blender, because the mortar and pestle bruises and crushes the ingredients instead of finely chopping them. Although this is better for releasing the aromas, it also results in a coarser texture. A food processor will quickly give you a nice smooth bumbu.

Below is a list of commonly used ingredients. They are readily available in the Netherlands and in the Flanders region of Belgium. In large cities, you can find them in Asian food stores or supermarkets. Most major supermarkets also carry a wide range of Asian ingredients. If you can't find something, don't worry—it doesn't have to be a disaster for your dish. Just look for an alternative. The result will be different, but also very tasty! After all, cooking often comes down to experimentation in the kitchen. For example, you can replace palm sugar with brown sugar. Many spices—like lemongrass, galangal, and ginger—are also available in powdered form. And the refreshing touch of makrut lime leaves can be replaced with some lime juice and grated lime zest.

BAWANG GORENG

Crispy fried shallots. Shallots fried in oil until golden brown and crispy. You can buy them in bags in Asian food stores, and nowadays they are also available in most supermarkets. They are especially delicious when sprinkled over a dish. The sweetish flavor of the shallots combines wonderfully with peanut sauce or nasi goreng (fried rice).

CREAMED COCONUT IN BLOCK FORM

Also known as santen, this thick, concentrated unsweetened creamed coconut is sold in a solid block. It is obtained by mixing grated coconut with hot water and reducing it. You can purchase blocks of creamed coconut in supermarkets and Asian food stores.

DJAHE

Ginger powder (ground dried ginger root). Recipes usually call for fresh ginger that is finely chopped or mashed into a paste. However, sometimes this can make the dish too wet or you might not want to have pieces of ginger in the dish. Ginger powder has the spicy flavor without the heat of fresh ginger.

DJERUK PURUT

Makrut lime leaves. The leaves of the makrut lime tree are either stewed whole in dishes or sauces or finely chopped and incorporated into bumbus. For the latter, you first need to remove the harder center rib. You usually buy them frozen. After thawing, they quickly become less aromatic. Keep in mind that you should put them in a well-sealed container if you want to store them in the refrigerator. Otherwise, everything in your fridge will take on the scent and taste of makrut lime leaves.

DJINTEN

Cumin powder (ground cumin seeds). It's even tastier, and quite easy, when you briefly toast cumin seeds in a dry skillet and then grind them into powder using a mortar and pestle.

EMPING

Melinjo nut crackers. These crackers have a nutty, slightly bitter, flavor. For vegans, they are a good alternative to krupuk (prawn crackers). They are delicious with sambal or just on their own with a bit of salt. You can also crumble them over salads for extra crunch.

GINGER ROOT

Fresh ginger root. Fresh ginger is used in many dishes for its wonderfully vibrant, peppery flavor. If you're cooking with fresh ginger, finely chop it first. You can also finely pound the chopped ginger in a mortar and pestle or include it in a bumbu. Although you can leave the skin on, peeling ensures that no bits of skin end up in the dish.

GULA DJAWA

Palm sugar. The sap of the sugar palm's blossom is boiled down into a thick brown syrup and poured into round molds, which then harden. Hollow bamboo stems are often used as molds. Gula djawa is sold in slices, with the bamboo still around them. You can chop the palm sugar with a chef's knife and mix it into a dish, or melt the slices in a small amount of water to make gula djawa syrup.

COMMON INGREDIENTS

KANGKUNG

Water spinach. A highly beloved vegetable in Indonesia, often quickly stir-fried and served as a side dish. The stems are a bit sturdier and require slightly longer cooking time than the leaves. Kangkung resembles spinach, although its taste is slightly more bitter. You can use a mixture of spinach and endive as a substitute.

KECAP

Kecap is soy sauce made from fermented soybeans, water, wheat, and salt. Kecap manis, or sweet soy sauce, also includes palm sugar. Some recipes require the use of thick kecap manis (ABC brand), which is more concentrated and syrupy. Try to use ABC brand if possible; it's readily available, and it tastes far better than other types of kecap.

KEMANGI

Lemon basil. Its leaves resemble regular basil, but are slightly elongated and pointed. It has a strongly lemony flavor, with a hint of anise. This herb pairs well with fish dishes.

KEMIRI NUTS

In English, they are called candlenuts; there is no translation in Dutch. They look similar to macadamia nuts and are widely used in bumbus. They provide thickness to a sauce and counterbalance the spiciness of peppers. Always roast them briefly in a skillet before using them, as they contain a mildly toxic substance when raw.

KENCUR

Kencur powder (ground dried kencur root, also known as aromatic ginger). Kencur root looks somewhat like turmeric and galangal in appearance but tastes completely different. Fresh kencur is sometimes used in Indonesia, but is hard to find in the Netherlands and Flanders. Take care and use sparingly, because the flavor is quite pronounced.

KETAN RICE

Sticky rice. This rice variety is sometimes also called glutinous rice, referring to its sticky nature. The rice contains lots of starch, which causes the grains to stick together. Use less water than usual when cooking this rice. For Indonesian *lemper*, the rice is steamed.

KETUMBAR

Coriander powder (ground coriander seeds). Its flavor is warm, spicy, and vibrant, and adds depth to a great many dishes.

KUNYIT

Turmeric powder (ground dried turmeric root). In Dutch, turmeric is also called "geelwortel" and is commonly known as "kurkuma." It is a primary component of curry powder. Turmeric has a mild, slightly bitter flavor, and is mainly used to impart color to dishes. When spilled onto clothing, it can leave yellow stains that are challenging to remove.

KUNYIT LEAF

Turmeric leaf (the leaf of the turmeric plant). It is used primarily in dishes from West Sumatra, and is added whole and stewed in the sauce to give it an extra spicy flavor. Turmeric leaf is difficult to find in the Netherlands and Flanders, although larger Asian food stores or supermarkets might sometimes have it. Alternatively, you can use a few slices of turmeric root instead.

LABU SIAM

Chayote. A green, pear-shaped fruit with a mild, fresh flavor that somewhat resembles cucumber and melon. Due to its mild flavor, it is also popular among children. Chayote is delicious in dishes like sayur. You can use zucchini as a substitute.

LAOS

Galangal root. Galangal resembles ginger, but has a milder, citrus-like flavor. Typically, fresh galangal is sliced and stewed in a dish or incorporated into a bumbu. Unlike fresh ginger, you should store this root in the refrigerator. It is also available in dried and powdered form.

LOMBOK

Spanish chili pepper. Lombok is the Indonesian name for red or green Spanish chili peppers. This pepper is relatively mild. The seeds and membranes are the hottest parts, which you can remove if you prefer less heat.

NANGKA

Jackfruit. This fruit is available in cans in Asian food stores. There are both non-sweet and sweet varieties. The non-sweet, young jackfruit is canned in lightly salted water for use in savory dishes. In terms of texture, it resembles shredded meat. The sweet, ripe jackfruit is canned in syrup and is suitable for desserts. The sweet variety has a mango- and pineapple-like flavor.

PANDAN

Pandan leaves are the long, narrow leaves of a palm-like plant. You can buy them frozen in Asian food stores. Fold them in half and tie them in a knot to stew them in dishes. In sweet dishes, pandan paste is often used. This bright green paste with pandan extract is available in small bottles, and will give your dishes a beautiful green color.

PETAI BEANS

Bitter beans. Also known as stink beans due to their strong odor and taste, which is somewhat garlic-like. They are delicious in sambal or dishes with tempeh. You can buy them frozen in small bags at Asian food stores.

RAWIT

Rawits are small, very hot green or red chili peppers. They are also known as African bird's eye chilies or pili-pili. You can buy them fresh or dried. The recipes in this book use fresh ones, but dried ones can also be used. Be careful and use them sparingly if you are not accustomed to spicy food. While some Indonesian dishes are supposed to be quite spicy, you can use one less chili pepper or replace the rawit with the less spicy Spanish pepper, using half a Spanish pepper for one rawit.

SALAM LEAF

Indonesian bay leaf. Although salam leaf is often called Indonesian bay leaf, the leaves resemble bay leaves only in appearance. Their flavor is fresh and mild, and is released when you cook the leaves in a dish.

■

SAMBAL ULEK

Sambal oelek, the simplest sambal there is. It's usually not eaten on its own but serves as a base for dishes. You can make it yourself or use store-bought varieties. The brand doesn't matter much, but be sure to check for excessive amounts of added flavorings and preservatives.

■

SEREH

Lemongrass. These are highly aromatic stalks from a type of grass. For the optimal release of their aroma it's best to bruise them before simmering: snap the stalks a few times or give them a few good taps with the blunt side of a knife. If you want to incorporate lemongrass into a bumbu, you should finely chop the stalk, or the texture of your bumbu will be stringy.

■

TEMPEH

Tempeh is made from fermented soybeans, which are compressed into a thick cake. Tempeh is most delicious when marinated and then fried until crispy, but you can also steam it or use it in stir-fry dishes.

■

TEPUNG HUN KWE

Mung bean flour. This flour is made from the same beans used for sprouting mung bean sprouts. It is often used in Indonesian cuisine to make puddings, and serves as the base for the green "beans" in cendol.

TURMERIC ROOT

Fresh turmeric. Finely ground fresh turmeric root is used in bumbus, while sliced turmeric root is stewed with dishes. Take care and use sparingly, because using too much turmeric can make a dish bitter.

■

VEGETARIAN MUSHROOM SAUCE

From the Lee Kum Kee brand and labeled as Mushroom Vegetarian Stir-Fry Sauce, this sauce is based on umami-rich shiitake mushrooms, and sometimes referred to in recipes as "vegetarian oyster sauce." It is an excellent vegan substitute for sauces that include animal ingredients (such as oyster sauce, fish sauce, or shrimp paste).

COOKING TECHNIQUES: TIPS & TRICKS

- All recipes serve 4 people unless otherwise specified.

- 1 tablespoon equals 15 milliliters, and 1 teaspoon equals 5 milliliters; these are standard leveled measurements.

- Before starting, carefully read the entire recipe to adequately prepare yourself and avoid surprises while cooking.

- Bumbu: Mortar and pestle, blender or food processor. Refer to the Common Ingredients section in the Introduction for a note on preparing a bumbu.

- Storing bumbu: Bumbus can be stored for an extended period of time. It's handy to prepare a larger quantity all at once, especially if you already have larger quantities of the ingredients on hand. Fry the entire quantity of bumbu in oil, put it in a jar, and pour in a thin layer of oil. Due to the use of chilies, salt, and oil in most bumbus, you can safely store them in the refrigerator for several weeks.

- Tahu (Indonesian) and tofu are two terms for the same ingredient: soy "cheese" made from soy milk.

- Bruise lemongrass stalks by striking them several times with the blunt side of a knife.

- The quality of the coconut milk is crucial to the final result of the dish. Therefore, we recommend using coconut milk from the Indonesian brand Kara.

- Wok: A good wok is crucial. Although it doesn't necessarily have to be an authentic Asian wok, it should preferably have a non-stick coating. A wok is also handy for deep-frying.

- Stir-frying versus sautéing: Stir-frying differs significantly from sautéing. Stir-frying ensures that the ingredients don't become overcooked and retain their texture while developing a delicious fried flavor. The secret is to turn up the heat very high, use plenty of oil, and quickly stir the ingredients using one or two spatulas as you cook. Make sure you have your ingredients sliced and measured out before stir-frying.

- When using wooden skewers, soak them in water first to prevent them from burning during grilling.

- Veggie or vegan—the terms can be confusing. Here's a clarification:

  — Veggie is a popular abbreviation for vegetarian. A vegetarian doesn't eat meat, fish, or poultry but does eat dairy and eggs.
  — A vegan only eats plant-based foods, and doesn't eat meat, fish, poultry, dairy, eggs, or honey.

HOW TO CREATE A VEGETARIAN OR VEGAN RICE TABLE

A *rijsttafel*—or "rice table"—starts, of course, with rice. Deliciously fragrant, well-cooked rice truly makes the meal. While many people in the Netherlands opt for nasi goreng (fried rice), in Indonesia, they typically use steamed white rice as the basis for a meal. You should be careful not to mix too many different flavors when making fried rice, as many dishes in the rice table already have distinct, rich sauces and spices themselves. Flavors might clash if you serve seasoned rice alongside these dishes. If you are serving simpler dishes, like stir-fried vegetables, then fried rice can be quite tasty. For special occasions, you can serve nasi kuning: rice flavored with coconut and turmeric.

When preparing a rice table, good planning is crucial. Create a step-by-step plan for all of the dishes. Some dishes can be prepared a day or two in advance and stored in the refrigerator—then all you need to do is reheat them. Some dishes, such as acar (Indonesian pickles), are even tastier if you prepare them well in advance because the flavors have more time to meld. You can also prepare bumbus (spice pastes) ahead of time. Make sure that when your guests arrive, you only need to reheat or finish dishes and sauces. A chafing dish is handy for this, as it allows you to keep sauces and dishes warm for a while.

Chef Hendra suggests the following dishes for a well-balanced vegetarian and vegan rice table, including an appetizer and a dessert:

VEGETARIAN RICE TABLE

APPETIZER

JAMUR BUNGKUS KAREE
Mushroom and leek spring rolls

RICE TABLE

TELOR KUNING
Eggs in a spicy coconut sauce

RENDANG NANGKA MUDA
Spicy stewed young jackfruit

GULAI BOERENKOOL
Spicy kale curry

OPOR TAHU TEMPE
Tofu and tempeh in a spicy, creamy sauce

PERKEDEL JAGUNG
Corn fritters

JAMUR MASAK WIJEN
Spicy sautéed mushrooms

PERKEDEL TAHU
Spicy tofu balls

NASI GORENG AND WHITE RICE
Fried rice with vegetables and egg, plus white rice

DESSERT

PUDING SANTAN PANDAN
Coconut pandan pudding

VEGAN RICE TABLE

APPETIZER

SOP TAHU SANTAN
Tofu, vegetable, and coconut soup

RICE TABLE

RENDANG NANGKA MUDA
Spicy stewed young jackfruit

SATE JAMUR
Mushroom satay

GULAI BOERENKOOL
Spicy kale curry

OPOR TAHU TEMPE
Tofu and tempeh in a spicy, creamy sauce

TAHU GORENG ASAM MANIS
Fried tofu with tamarind sauce

SOP SAYUR SANTAN
Vegetable coconut curry

SALAD TAHU JAMUR
Spicy salad with tofu and various kinds of mushrooms

JAMUR MASAK WIJEN
Spicy sautéed mushrooms

NASI KUNING AND WHITE RICE
Yellow coconut rice, plus white rice

DESSERT

KUE UBI MANIS
Indonesian sweet potato pancakes

THE TEAM AT
RESTAURANT BLAUW

HENDRA SUBANDRIO

Hendra is the executive chef at both Blauw restaurants. This means he is in charge of the daily operations, manages the kitchen, develops recipes, and creates menus such as the rice tables. Initially, the menus of the restaurants differed slightly, but now both restaurants have the same menu. The emphasis is on authentic Indonesian cuisine. "In Indonesia, people eat rice with one or just a few dishes. However, during celebrations the table is filled with dishes, and that's when you have an XXL rice table."
Whenever Hendra talks about Indonesia or Restaurant Blauw, his eyes light up and he gets a smile on his face. It's clear where his heart and passion lie.

Hendra hails from Jakarta and speaks the dialect from there, which is different from Bahasa Indonesia. He mentions that as a child, like most other children, he gradually learned to adapt to spicy food. "Bit by bit, the food became spicier, and you get used to it."
In the Blauw kitchen, there are Indonesians as well as people from other countries like Thailand, Eritrea, and the Netherlands. "Indonesians speak Indonesian among themselves, but when others are present, we switch to Dutch or English. It's important to me that no one feels excluded," Hendra says. "We're one team, with one goal: to prepare the most delicious food. A sense of family among the staff makes it easier to achieve that goal."

YOU CAN FIND HENDRA'S RECIPES ON PAGES **73, 89, 91, 93, 133** AND **201.**

YUNITA DIRMAYANTI

Yunita is new at Blauw but is learning very quickly.

HENDRA SUBANDRIO

I chose the recipes for this book because they are my favorites.
They remind me of my mother and grandmother who used to cook these dishes for me.
Now that I live and work far away from them, I miss their food and the love they put into it.
By including these particular recipes in this cookbook, I want to honor them
and let them know how proud I am of them and how much I miss them.

YUNITA DIRMAYANTI

YOU CAN FIND YUNITA'S RECIPES ON PAGES **76, 84, 124, 126, 162, 170** AND **198**.

UMA PHETKAW

No one can roll spring rolls as quickly as Uma.
HENDRA SUBANDRIO

*The recipes I have chosen are healthy and delicious.
There are some dishes with tofu that help reduce bad cholesterol in the body.
My recipes show how to prepare tofu in a tasty way.*
UMA PHETKAW

YOU CAN FIND UMA'S RECIPES ON PAGES **64, 68, 112, 128, 178, 186, 190** AND **192**.

DONNI SETIAWAN SUGANDA

*For Donni, it's all about having a good time—to him, an enjoyable work environment is essential.
And he certainly contributes to the cheerful atmosphere.*

HENDRA SUBANDRIO

*I've chosen recipes that my mother and grandmother used to make.
I always found them delicious and have beautiful memories of them.
Now that I live in the Netherlands, I miss these dishes; I sometimes prepare them for myself.
Sometimes I ask my mother for tips when I'm making them.*

DONNI SETIAWAN SUGANDA

YOU CAN FIND DONNI'S RECIPES ON PAGES 94, 102, 110, 142, 144, 204 AND 206.

MULFI YASIR

No frowning, just frying: this suits Mulfi to a tee.
HENDRA SUBANDRIO

During my hotel management studies, I learned about Indonesian cuisine.
Since then, I've been cooking and experimenting on my own.
I mostly prepare vegetarian dishes because I want to show people how delicious meals
can be without using meat, fish, or poultry—it's much tastier than most people realize.
MULFI YASIR

YOU CAN FIND MULFI'S RECIPES ON PAGES **62**, **100**, **114**, **138**, **148**, **184** AND **208**.

FELIX PONTOH

Felix has been with us the longest—he's been a permanent member of the Blauw team for seventeen years.

HENDRA SUBANDRIO

I've chosen dishes that my mother always cooked, and I have very fond memories of them.

FELIX PONTOH

YOU CAN FIND FELIX'S RECIPES ON PAGES **104** AND **106**.

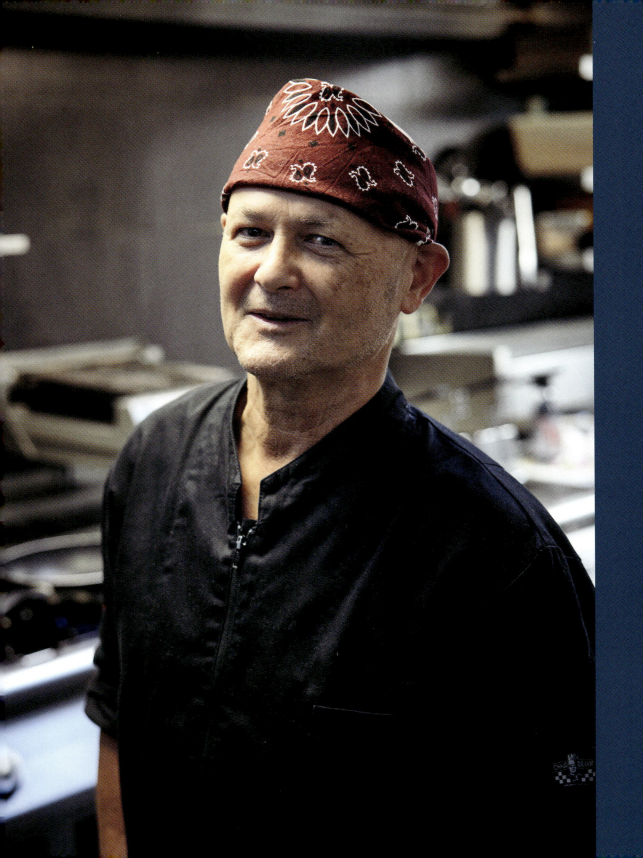

MICHEL E SALEH

The oldest employee, but with the youngest spirit.

HENDRA SUBANDRIO

Indonesian cuisine is well-suited to vegetarian cooking and eating.
I myself am fond of tofu and tempeh. My recipe for bami is delicious, full of vegetables,
and not only vegan but also gluten-free. I found that to be a fun challenge, and I really enjoy it myself.
I chose the croquette because Dutch people love croquettes. The filling is made from sayur lodeh.

MICHEL E SALEH

YOU CAN FIND MICHEL'S RECIPES ON PAGES **74** AND **134**.

DEWI PETERS

Our quiet strength behind the scenes.
HENDRA SUBANDRIO

For me, the recipes I've chosen are cherished childhood memories.
For example, my father, who was a trader, used to bring wingko Babat home.
DEWI PETERS

YOU CAN FIND DEWI'S RECIPES ON PAGES **86, 120** AND **210**.

VERA ATIKA

*Vera looks out for everyone she works with:
she's like a caring mother in our kitchen.*

HENDRA SUBANDRIO

*My mother is a good cook. She cooks with simple herbs.
Now I cook in the same way for my children, and they also love that kind of food.
That's why I'm sharing these recipes in this book: the dishes are simple, healthy, and delicious.*

VERA ATIKA

YOU CAN FIND VERA'S RECIPES ON PAGES **96, 108, 176** AND **180**.

PETER DE GROOT

Peter is cheerful, laughs a lot, and is always singing—
that's why it's so pleasant to work with him.

HENDRA SUBANDRIO

All of the recipes I share in this book remind me of Java.
When I was eighteen, I moved to the big city, Yogyakarta.
I was surprised and amazed by the enormous variety of food available everywhere.
I found it inspiring that you can cook so many different things.

PETER DE GROOT

YOU CAN FIND PETER'S RECIPES ON PAGES **80, 98, 156** AND **160**.

TIRTA SULAMIT

Tirta loves cooking, but she loves eating even more.
HENDRA SUBANDRIO

These dishes bring back old memories of my childhood.
Every time I make them, I feel like a child again.
TIRTA SULAMIT

YOU CAN FIND TIRTA'S RECIPES ON PAGES **78, 82, 116, 118, 154** AND **196.**

THE TEAM AT RESTAURANT BLAUW

SOUPS

SAYUR ASEM

Tamarind soup

■

Sayur asem is a tangy vegetarian vegetable soup flavored with tamarind. While our first restaurant cookbook ("Blauw: Authentic Indonesian Dishes," in Dutch) also includes a recipe for this beloved soup, this version offers a different yet equally delicious take on it.

MULFI YASIR

 MAIN COURSE   VEGAN   SERVES 4   MULFI YASIR

1½ liters water
2 ears of sweet corn
100 g yard-long beans
100 g Chinese cabbage or white cabbage
1 chayote (labu siam)
1 red bell pepper
50 g unsalted peanuts, finely chopped

SAUCE
3 candlenuts (kemiri nuts)
4 garlic cloves, peeled
3 red Spanish chili peppers (lombok), chopped
3 Indonesian bay leaves (salam leaves)
3 cm fresh galangal (laos), peeled and sliced
200 ml tamarind water
2 teaspoons salt
25 g palm sugar (gula djawa)

1. Start by bringing the water to a boil in a large soup pot.

2. Meanwhile, roast the candlenuts in a dry frying pan for 1 to 2 minutes.

3. Grind the candlenuts, garlic, and chopped chilies into a bumbu (spice paste) using a food processor or mortar and pestle. Add this bumbu to the boiling water along with the other sauce ingredients. Stir well, reduce the heat, and simmer gently while you prepare the vegetables.

4. Cut the kernels from the corn cobs with a sharp knife, add them to the broth, and let them cook for 5 minutes.

5. Trim the ends of the yard-long beans and cut the pods into 3-cm pieces. Slice the cabbage into thin strips and dice the chayote into 1 x 1-cm cubes. Remove the seeds from the bell pepper and slice it into strips. Add these prepared vegetables to the tamarind broth. Allow to simmer gently for another 3 to 5 minutes.

6. Finally, ladle the soup into bowls or serving dishes and garnish with the chopped peanuts.

SOUPS

SOP JAMUR

Spicy mushroom broth

∎

This is a delicious and spicy mushroom broth.
UMA PHETKAW

 STARTER OR MAIN COURSE   VEGAN   SERVES 2 OR 4   UMA PHETKAW

500 ml water
40 g fresh galangal (laos), peeled and sliced
40 g lemongrass (sereh), sliced
8 makrut lime leaves (djeruk purut)
2 spring onions (scallions), sliced diagonally
10 g bird's-eye chilies (rawit), sliced diagonally
200 g oyster mushrooms, torn into pieces
250 g white mushrooms, sliced
150 g small tomatoes, halved
1 tablespoon tamarind water
4 tablespoons light soy sauce
50 g sugar
1 teaspoon salt
½ vegetable bouillon cube
50 ml lemon juice
15 g cilantro, coarsely chopped

1. Put the water in a soup pot and add the galangal, lemongrass, makrut lime leaves, spring onions, and bird's eye chili. Bring to a boil.

2. When the water boils, add the oyster mushrooms, white mushrooms, and tomatoes. Stir well. Add the tamarind water, soy sauce, sugar, salt, and vegetable bouillon cube. Simmer for 2 minutes.

3. Turn off the heat and add the lemon juice and cilantro.

4. Serve with white rice.

SOP LABU

Pumpkin soup

∎

Indonesian cuisine also features pumpkin soup, slightly spicy and with a refreshing touch of lemongrass and makrut lime leaves.

 STARTER   VEGAN   SERVES 4   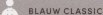 BLAUW CLASSIC

2 tablespoons oil
1 onion, peeled and chopped
2 garlic cloves, finely chopped
1 red Spanish chili pepper (lombok), finely chopped
5 cm ginger, peeled and finely chopped
1 teaspoon ground coriander (ketumbar)
1 lemongrass (sereh) stalk, cut into pieces and bruised
3 makrut lime leaves (djeruk purut)
800 g pumpkin, diced
600 ml vegetable broth
200 ml coconut milk
pepper and salt
1 lime

1. Heat the oil in a soup pan and sauté the onion, garlic, red chili, and ginger, stirring, for 5 minutes.

2. Add the coriander and stir-fry for 1 minute.

3. Put the lemongrass, makrut lime leaves, and pumpkin in the pan, then add the vegetable broth. Stir, bring to a boil, and simmer gently for 20 minutes.

4. Remove the pan from the heat. Take out the lemongrass and makrut lime leaves, then puree the soup with a hand blender until smooth.

5. Mix the coconut milk into the soup and warm it briefly. Avoid boiling to prevent the coconut milk from curdling.

6. Season with pepper and salt, and a squeeze of lime juice.

SOP TAHU SANTAN

Tofu coconut soup

■

*A fantastically tasty, spicy soup with vegetables, tofu, and coconut.
Serve this soup with white rice if you want to make it a main course.*
UMA PHETKAW

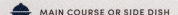 MAIN COURSE OR SIDE DISH   VEGAN   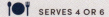 SERVES 4 OR 6   UMA PHETKAW

250 ml coconut milk
200 ml water
1 vegetable bouillon cube
8 makrut lime leaves (djeruk purut)
30 g fresh galangal (laos), peeled and thinly sliced
40 g lemongrass (sereh), sliced
150 g tofu, cut into 1 x 1-cm cubes
100 g mushrooms, sliced
200 g tomatoes, quartered
50 g carrots, diced
15 g cilantro, coarsely chopped
1 tablespoon tamarind water
30 g red Spanish chili peppers (lombok), sliced
4 teaspoons mushroom soy sauce
2 teaspoons salt
3 tablespoons lemon juice

1. In a large pan, combine the coconut milk, water, bouillon cube, makrut lime leaves, galangal, and lemongrass. Stir and bring to a boil.

2. Once the coconut broth is boiling, add the tofu, mushrooms, tomatoes, and carrots. Stir well and bring back to a boil. Once it boils, add the cilantro, tamarind water, red chilies, and mushroom soy sauce. Simmer for 2 minutes.

3. Season with salt. Turn off the heat and stir in the lemon juice.

MAIN COURSES

ASEM PADE NANGKA MUDA

Jackfruit in a spiced sauce

Jackfruit is well-suited for using in vegetarian cuisine. Its texture resembles meat, and its neutral flavor readily absorbs other flavors.
HENDRA SUBANDRIO

 MAIN COURSE   VEGAN   SERVES 4   HENDRA SUBANDRIO

3 tablespoons oil
1 onion, peeled and chopped
2 garlic cloves, finely chopped
1 lemongrass (sereh) stalk, cut into quarters and bruised
1 tablespoon sambal oelek
1 turmeric leaf (kunyit leaf), sliced
200 ml water
2 tablespoons tamarind water
600 g young jackfruit (nangka), cut into smaller pieces if desired
freshly ground pepper and salt

BUMBU
3 red Spanish chili peppers (lombok), chopped
3 bird's eye chilies (rawit), chopped
½ red bell pepper, chopped
5 cm fresh ginger, peeled and chopped
5 cm fresh turmeric, peeled and chopped
5 cm fresh galangal (laos), peeled and chopped
3 candlenuts (kemiri nuts), chopped
½ teaspoon salt

1. Grind all of the ingredients for the bumbu into a smooth paste using a food processor.

2. Heat the oil in a wok and sauté the onion and garlic for 2 minutes. Add the bumbu and stir-fry for another 3 minutes.

3. Add the lemongrass, sambal oelek, and turmeric leaf to the bumbu mixture in the pan and pour in the water. Stir well and let the sauce simmer gently for 10 minutes. Add a little extra water if necessary; the sauce should have the consistency of soup.

4. Stir in the tamarind water and add the jackfruit. Simmer over low heat for another 10 to 15 minutes.

5. Season with pepper and salt.

BAMI TIMUN JEPANG

Noodles made from zucchini

Zucchini cut into ribbons can be prepared like noodles.
MICHEL E SALEH

 MAIN COURSE   VEGAN   SERVES 4   MICHEL E SALEH

2 zucchinis
2 to 3 tablespoons oil
6 makrut lime leaves (djeruk purut)
2 tablespoons vegetable broth
soy sauce
pepper and salt
1 tablespoon finely chopped parsley
2 spring onions (scallions), sliced
1 egg per person, boiled or fried (optional, for a vegetarian version)

BUMBU
2 onions, peeled and coarsely chopped
8 garlic cloves, peeled
4 red Spanish chili peppers (lombok), chopped
100 g fresh ginger, peeled and chopped

ADDITIONAL EQUIPMENT
spiralizer

1. Grind the ingredients for the bumbu into a paste using a food processor or mortar and pestle.

2. Using a spiralizer, cut the zucchini into noodle-like ribbons.

3. Heat the oil in a wok and sauté the bumbu, stirring constantly.

4. After 3 minutes, add the zucchini and makrut lime leaves. Stir-fry for 2 minutes.

5. Season with the vegetable broth, soy sauce, pepper, and salt.

6. Turn off the heat and garnish with the parsley and spring onions. If you like you can also add two slices of grilled zucchini.

7. Serve the "noodles" with boiled or fried eggs, if desired.

BIHUN GORENG KAMPUNG

Stir-fried thin rice noodles

■

*This dish of stir-fried noodles is prepared slightly differently in every family.
But all of these different versions have one thing in common: they're always tasty.*
YUNITA DIRMAYANTI

 MAIN COURSE   VEGETARIAN   🍴 SERVES 4   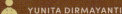 YUNITA DIRMAYANTI

200 g rice vermicelli
4 tablespoons sweet soy sauce (kecap manis)
3 tablespoons oil
2 eggs
6 garlic cloves, finely chopped
1 medium carrot, coarsely grated
50 g Chinese cabbage, thinly sliced
freshly ground white pepper and salt
1 teaspoon sugar
2 spring onions (scallions), sliced (including the green part)
½ tablespoon finely chopped celery leaves

1. Prepare the rice vermicelli according to the package instructions. Drain, then mix in the sweet soy sauce and set aside.

2. Heat the oil in a wok. Beat the eggs, add them to the wok, and stir-fry to scramble. Add the garlic and stir-fry.

3. Add the carrot and stir-fry for 1 minute. Add the Chinese cabbage and stir-fry for another 2 minutes.

4. Add the rice vermicelli, pepper and salt, and sugar, and stir well. Mix in the spring onions and turn off the heat. Garnish with the chopped celery leaves.

BUBUR MANADO / TINUTUAN

Spiced rice with vegetables

∎

I come from Manado, the capital of North Sulawesi.
There, I had Manado porridge for breakfast every day. Delicious with a cup of hot tea.
TIRTA SULAMIT

 MAIN COURSE   VEGAN   SERVES 4   TIRTA SULAMIT

1 bunch of water spinach (kangkung)
250 g cassava
500 g pumpkin
2 liters water
100 g rice
300 g canned corn kernels
2 lemongrass (sereh) stalks, bruised
2 turmeric leaves (kunyit leaves)
salt
2 spring onions (scallions), finely chopped
1 bunch Thai basil, coarsely chopped
1 teaspoon fried garlic
2 tablespoons crispy fried shallots (bawang goreng)
fried tofu, to serve
hot chili sauce, to serve

1. Wash the water spinach and cut it into narrow strips.

2. Peel the cassava and remove the skin from the pumpkin. Cut the flesh of both into small cubes, 1 x 1 cm.

3. Put the water in a large pan and add the cassava, pumpkin, rice, corn kernels, lemongrass, and turmeric leaves. Stir and bring to a boil, then cook for about 25 min. Now mash the pumpkin with a fork, spoon, or masher so that the rice turns orange.

4. Add the sliced water spinach and mix well.

5. Season with salt. Stir in the spring onions, basil, fried garlic, and crispy fried shallots.

6. Serve with fried tofu and hot chili sauce.

CAGER TELUR MADURA

Fried eggs in a spicy sauce

∎

Madura is an island to the north of East Java.
PETER DE GROOT

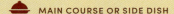 MAIN COURSE OR SIDE DISH   VEGETARIAN   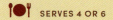 SERVES 4 OR 6   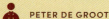 PETER DE GROOT

300 ml oil, for deep-frying
8 hard-boiled eggs, peeled
50 ml oil, for stir-frying the bumbu
10 makrut lime leaves (djeruk purut)
30 g vegetable bouillon powder
pinch of sugar
salt, to taste
200 ml water
300 g white cabbage, finely chopped
60 g red Spanish chili peppers (lombok), sliced diagonally

BUMBU
150 g shallots, peeled and chopped
20 g garlic, finely chopped
50 g candlenuts (kemiri nuts), chopped
5 g turmeric powder (kunyit)
30 g fresh ginger, peeled and finely chopped
40 g fresh galangal (laos), peeled and finely chopped

1. Heat the oil for deep-frying to 160 °C. Fry the eggs in the hot oil until they are golden brown, about 2 minutes on each side. Remove them from the pan and set aside.

2. Grind the ingredients for the bumbu into a paste using a food processor or mortar and pestle.

3. Heat the 50 ml of oil in a wok over medium heat, add the bumbu and makrut lime leaves, and stir-fry for 3 minutes, until fragrant.

4. Add the vegetable bouillon powder, sugar, salt to taste, and water; stir and bring to a boil.

5. Add the eggs, stir gently, and cook for about 5 minutes.

6. Add the cabbage and red chilies, and cook for another 5 minutes.

7. Transfer to a serving dish and enjoy!

SOP SAYUR SANTAN

Vegetable coconut curry

∎

This is a delightful spicy curry made with vegetables and coconut.
TIRTA SULAMIT

 MAIN COURSE   VEGAN   SERVES 2   TIRTA SULAMIT

1 tablespoon oil
1 onion, peeled and chopped
1 tomato, finely chopped
1 green Spanish chili pepper (lombok), finely chopped
1 teaspoon garlic powder
1 teaspoon ground ginger (djahe)
½ teaspoon paprika
½ teaspoon ground cumin (djinten)
2 Maggi bouillon cubes
1 teaspoon tomato paste
2 potatoes, peeled and diced
120 g peas (frozen)
50 g carrots, diced
200 ml water
120 ml coconut cream
juice of 1 lemon
salt

1. Heat the oil in a pan and sauté the onion until it starts to color.

2. Add the tomato and stir-fry until it softens.

3. Mix in the green chili, garlic powder, ground ginger, paprika, ground cumin, Maggi cubes, and tomato paste, stirring well.

4. Add the potatoes, peas, carrots, and water. Stir well, cover with a lid, and bring to a boil. Cook until the potatoes are tender.

5. Stir in the coconut cream, mix well, and warm gently for another 2 minutes.

6. Mix in the lemon juice and serve. Season with salt if necessary.

GULAI BOERENKOOL

Spicy kale curry

This version of kale might be lesser-known, but it's incredibly delicious. "Boerenkool" is kale in English.
YUNITA DIRMAYANTI

 MAIN COURSE   VEGAN   SERVES 4    YUNITA DIRMAYANTI

2 tablespoons oil
1 lemongrass (sereh) stalk, bruised
2 cm fresh galangal (laos), peeled and chopped
800 ml thin coconut milk
200 g kale, stems removed and finely chopped
1 teaspoon salt
2 teaspoons sugar

BUMBU
2 shallots, peeled
2 garlic cloves, peeled
1 teaspoon ground coriander (ketumbar)
½ teaspoon turmeric powder (kunyit)
1 candlenut (kemiri nut)
2 red Spanish chili peppers (lombok), chopped

1. Grind the ingredients for the bumbu into a paste using a food processor or mortar and pestle.

2. Heat the oil in a wok and sauté the bumbu with the lemongrass and galangal, stirring constantly, until fragrant and starting to color.

3. Add the coconut milk and stir as it comes to a boil. Then add the kale and cook for another 2 to 3 minutes.

4. Season with salt and sugar.

JAMUR MASAK WIJEN

Sesame-flavored sautéed mushrooms

∎

Indonesian cuisine also incorporates influences from other Asian countries like China, India, and Japan. This recipe has Chinese-Indonesian origins, and is quick to make.

DEWI PETERS

 MAIN COURSE   VEGAN   SERVES 2   DEWI PETERS

4 tablespoons sunflower oil
2 garlic cloves, finely chopped
100 g mushrooms, halved
1 teaspoon ground white pepper
2 cm fresh ginger, grated
1 tablespoon sweet soy sauce (kecap manis)
1 tablespoon soy sauce (kecap asin)
salt
2 spring onions (scallions), sliced diagonally
1 tablespoon sesame oil
2 tablespoons sesame seeds

1. Heat the sunflower oil in a wok or deep fryer. Briefly sauté the garlic. Add the mushrooms and stir-fry for 2 minutes, stirring constantly. Do not cook longer, as the mushrooms should remain firm.

2. Add the white pepper, ginger, sweet soy sauce, soy sauce, and salt to taste. Add the spring onions and sesame oil. Stir-fry over high heat for another 30 seconds.

3. Transfer to a serving dish and garnish with the sesame seeds.

4. Serve with rice or noodles.

MAIN COURSES

87

KWETIEUW SAYUR

Rice noodles with vegetables

■

A delightful noodle dish packed with vegetables.
HENDRA SUBANDRIO

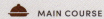 MAIN COURSE   VEGETARIAN   SERVES 4   HENDRA SUBANDRIO

200 g flat rice noodles
4 tablespoons oil, plus a splash more
200 g mushrooms, thinly sliced
3 garlic cloves, finely chopped
4 eggs, beaten with pepper and salt
4 spring onions (scallions), sliced
2 red Spanish chili peppers (lombok) sliced
400 g choi sam or bok choy, cut into pieces
400 g pointed cabbage, thinly sliced
1 tablespoon sambal oelek
150 g bean sprouts
sweet soy sauce (kecap manis)
vegetarian oyster sauce
pepper and salt

1. Place the rice noodles in a bowl. Pour in an ample amount of boiling water and let them soak for 2 to 3 minutes. Drain in a colander and rinse with cold water. Add a splash of oil to prevent sticking.

2. Heat the 4 tablespoons of oil in a wok. Make sure you have two spatulas and all of the ingredients ready.

3. Stir-fry the mushrooms and garlic in the wok until the garlic turns golden. Then add the egg to the wok and stir. The heat will cause the egg to quickly set into an omelet.

4. Add the spring onions, red chilies, choi sam, and pointed cabbage. Stir-fry everything over medium-high heat for 2 to 3 minutes. Then add the sambal oelek and rice noodles and stir-fry for another 2 to 3 minutes.

5. Finally, add the bean sprouts along with the sweet soy sauce and vegetarian oyster sauce. Heat for another 1 minute. Adjust the seasoning by adding more pepper and salt if necessary.

MAIN COURSES

LODEH TEMPE PETE

Tempeh stewed in coconut milk

Petai beans, also known as bitter beans, can be roasted in their pods and then peeled. Here, though, we cut the beans into strips and sauté them in oil.

HENDRA SUBANDRIO

 MAIN COURSE OR SIDE DISH   VEGAN   SERVES 4 OR 6   HENDRA SUBANDRIO

3 tablespoons oil
200 g tempeh, cut into 1 x 3-cm strips
1 green Spanish chili pepper (lombok), sliced
50 g petai beans (bitter beans), sliced
1 teaspoon sambal oelek
200 ml water
200 ml coconut milk
pepper and salt
1 spring onion (scallion), sliced

BUMBU
1 onion, peeled and chopped
2 garlic cloves, peeled
1 tomato, chopped
vegetable bouillon powder, to taste

1. Grind the ingredients for the bumbu into a smooth paste using a food processor or mortar and pestle.

2. Heat the oil in a heavy-bottomed pan and sauté the bumbu for 5 minutes, stirring constantly.

3. Add the tempeh strips and sauté for 3 to 5 minutes until brown.

4. Add the green chili, petai beans, and sambal oelek and sauté for 1 minute. Pour in the water, stir, and bring to a boil. Simmer for 5 minutes.

5. Add the coconut milk, heat briefly, and season with pepper and salt.

6. Garnish with the spring onion.

NANGKA RICA RICA

Jackfruit in a spicy sauce

■

Jackfruit has a neutral flavor, which makes it perfect for using with seasonings that have a spicy kick.
HENDRA SUBANDRIO

 MAIN COURSE   VEGAN   SERVES 4   HENDRA SUBANDRIO

5 tablespoons oil
1 large onion, peeled and chopped
2 lemongrass (sereh) stalks, cut into pieces and bruised
3 makrut lime leaves (djeruk purut)
2 Indonesian bay leaves (salam leaves)
2 tomatoes
600 g young jackfruit (nangka)
salt (optional)
a few sprigs of lemon basil (kemangi), finely chopped

BUMBU
5 cm fresh ginger, peeled and chopped
5 cm fresh galangal (laos), peeled and sliced
2 garlic cloves, peeled
½ red bell pepper, chopped
3 red bird's-eye chilies (rawit), chopped
1 red Spanish chili pepper (lombok), chopped
1 teaspoon salt

1. Coarsely grind all of the ingredients for the bumbu in a food processor.

2. Heat the oil in a wok and sauté the onion until translucent. Add the bumbu, lemongrass, makrut lime leaves, and Indonesian bay leaves, and stir-fry for 10 minutes.

3. Cut a cross into the bottom of the tomatoes. Immerse them in boiling water for 30 seconds, then remove the skin. Chop the tomatoes into small pieces.

4. Add the jackfruit to the bumbu, stir-fry briefly, then add the tomatoes. Reduce the heat and simmer gently for 15 minutes.

5. Season with salt if necessary, and sprinkle with finely chopped lemon basil before serving.

OPOR TAHU TEMPE

Tofu and tempeh in a spicy, creamy sauce

Tofu and tempeh in a spicy, creamy sauce. Mmmmmmm. Delicious!
DONNI SETIAWAN SUGANDA

 MAIN COURSE   VEGETARIAN   SERVES 4    DONNI SETIAWAN SUGANDA

250 g tofu
250 g tempeh
3 tablespoons oil
2 lemongrass (sereh) stalks, bruised
5 makrut lime leaves (djeruk purut)
3 Indonesian bay leaves (salam leaves)
1 teaspoon ground white pepper
1 tablespoon salt
1 teaspoon sugar
1 teaspoon vegetable bouillon powder
1½ liters water
250 ml coconut milk

BUMBU
6 garlic cloves, peeled
8 shallots, peeled
6 cm fresh ginger, peeled and sliced
6 cm fresh galangal (laos), peeled and sliced
1 teaspoon ground coriander (ketumbar)
4 candlenuts (kemiri nuts)

1. Cut the tofu and tempeh into 1½ x 1½-cm cubes. Set aside.

2. Grind the ingredients for the bumbu into a paste using a food processor or mortar and pestle.

3. Heat the oil in a pan and stir-fry the bumbu for 2 to 3 minutes until fragrant.

4. Add the lemongrass, makrut lime leaves, Indonesian bay leaves, white pepper, salt, sugar, and vegetable bouillon powder. Mix well.

5. Add the water and coconut milk and stir well. Bring to a boil.

6. Stir in the tofu and tempeh, reduce the heat, and simmer for another 5 to 10 minutes.

OSENG TEMPE

Stir-fried tempeh

■

"Oseng" refers to stir-frying, a cooking technique commonly used in Indonesian cooking. The word that follows indicates the stir-fried ingredient (or one of the stir-fried ingredients), in this case, tempeh.

VERA ATIKA

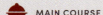 MAIN COURSE   VEGAN   SERVES 4   VERA ATIKA

150 ml oil

400 g tempeh, cut into 2 x 2-cm cubes

180 g onions, finely chopped

40 g garlic, thinly sliced

5 red Spanish chili peppers (lombok), thinly sliced

1 beefsteak tomato, diced

3 makrut lime leaves (djeruk purut)

4 generous tablespoons sweet soy sauce (kecap manis)

1 teaspoon salt

5 teaspoons sugar

1. Heat 100 ml of the oil in a frying pan. Fry the tempeh cubes until they are golden brown and crispy. Remove from the pan and set aside.

2. Heat the remaining oil in the pan and sauté the onions, garlic, red chilies, tomato, and makrut lime leaves over high heat for 5 minutes, stirring constantly. Reduce the heat after 5 minutes, add the tempeh, and stir to combine.

3. Add the sweet soy sauce, salt, and sugar, stir, and simmer for another 4 to 5 minutes.

PEPES TAHU BETAWI

Steamed tofu in banana leaves

∎

*I tried Pepes tahu Betawi for the first time in Yogyakarta.
This dish was remarkably delicious!*
PETER DE GROOT

 MAIN COURSE   VEGAN   SERVES 4   PETER DE GROOT

30 ml oil, for frying
5 g turmeric powder (kunyit)
10 g ground coriander (ketumbar)
2 lemongrass (sereh) stalks, just the white part, sliced diagonally into 2-cm pieces
5 g makrut lime leaves (djeruk purut), torn in half
100 g tomatoes, diced
5 g bird's eye chilies (rawit), finely chopped (optional)
salt
30 g ground white pepper
5 g vegetable bouillon powder
300 g oyster mushrooms, chopped
a handful of lemon basil (kemangi) leaves
100 g spring onions (scallions), sliced
400 g firm tofu, mashed
2 eggs, beaten

BUMBU (SPICE PASTE)
30 g garlic, finely chopped
200 g shallots, peeled and finely chopped
50 g candlenuts (kemiri nuts), chopped
100 g red chilies, chopped

ADDITIONAL EQUIPMENT
10 banana leaves, 20 x 20 cm
wooden cocktail sticks

1. Grind the ingredients for the bumbu into a paste using a food processor.

2. Heat the oil in a wok over medium-high heat and stir-fry the kunyit and ketumbar until fragrant.

3. Add the lemongrass and makrut lime leaves and stir-fry for about 2 minutes.

4. Add the diced tomatoes and the bird's eye chilies, if using, and continue to stir-fry. Season with salt to taste, turmeric, coriander, white pepper, and vegetable bouillon powder.

5. Add the oyster mushrooms, mix well, and stir-fry for another 1 minute.

6. Turn off the heat. Add the lemon basil, spring onions, mashed tofu, and beaten eggs. Mix everything thoroughly.

7. Place a banana leaf on a cutting board and spoon on 2 to 3 tablespoons of the tofu mixture. Fold the banana leaf around this filling to make a packet, and fasten each end with a wooden cocktail stick. Make packets from the rest of the banana leaves and filling in the same way.

8. Steam the packets in the steamer for about 30 minutes.

9. Grill the packets in a non-stick grill pan for 3 to 4 minutes on each side just before serving.

RENDANG NANGKA MUDA

Spicy stewed young jackfruit

■

Rendang is traditionally made with beef, but it's also delicious with young jackfruit, making it suitable for vegetarians and vegans.
MULFI YASIR

 MAIN COURSE   VEGAN   SERVES 4 OR 5   MULFI YASIR

400 ml coconut milk
100 g creamed coconut (from a block)
100 g grated dried coconut
1 kg young jackfruit (nangka)

SAUCE
100 g red Spanish chili peppers (lombok)
1 kg onions, peeled and chopped
10 garlic cloves, peeled
10 cm fresh ginger, peeled and chopped
50 g fresh galangal (laos), peeled and sliced
200 ml oil
30 g turmeric leaves (kunyit leaves)
5 lemongrass (sereh) stalks
20 g Indonesian bay leaves (salam leaves)
30 g makrut lime leaves (djeruk purut)
2 tablespoons salt
3 tablespoons ground black pepper
5 tablespoons sambal oelek
100 g candlenuts (kemiri nuts)
3 cinnamon sticks
2 star anise
1 teaspoon ground nutmeg
2 tablespoons ground coriander (ketumbar)
2 teaspoons turmeric powder (kunyit)
2 tablespoons ground cumin (djinten)
2 teaspoons ground cardamom

1. For the sauce, grind the red chilies, onions, garlic, ginger, and galangal into a bumbu using a food processor.

2. Heat the oil in a large wok and stir-fry the bumbu until it is fragrant and changes color.

3. Add the remaining sauce ingredients and mix well. Add the coconut milk, creamed coconut, and grated coconut. Simmer over low heat until the sauce thickens. Stir regularly to prevent the coconut milk from splitting.

4. Cut the jackfruit into small pieces and add them to the sauce. Simmer for another 5 to 10 minutes.

SAMBAL GORENG TAHU KENTANG

Kruidig gebakken tofu en aardappel

∎

This version of fried tofu and potatoes is super tasty and truly my favorite.
DONNI SETIAWAN SUGANDA

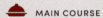 MAIN COURSE   VEGAN   SERVES 4   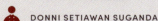 DONNI SETIAWAN SUGANDA

350 g tofu
200 g potatoes
oil for deep-frying
10 shallots, peeled
5 garlic cloves
5 petai beans (bitter beans)
2 red bell peppers, diced
1 tomato, diced
250 ml water
1 teaspoon salt
2 tablespoons sugar
¼ vegetable bouillon cube or
  1 teaspoon vegetable bouillon powder
2 teaspoons tamarind water

1. Cut the tofu into 2 x 2-cm cubes.

2. Peel the potatoes and cut them into 2 x 2-cm cubes. Make sure the cubes are not wet; pat them dry with paper towels if necessary.

3. Heat a generous amount of oil in a wok and fry the tofu cubes until golden brown. Remove them from the pan and drain on paper towels.

4. Reheat the oil, adding extra oil if necessary, and fry the potato cubes until golden brown and cooked through, about 5 to 7 minutes. Remove the potatoes from the pan and drain on paper towels.

5. Chop the shallots and finely chop the garlic. Heat 2 tablespoons oil in another pan and sauté the shallots, garlic, and petai beans, stirring constantly, for 3 to 5 minutes. Add the bell pepper and tomato and sauté for another 3 minutes, stirring regularly.

6. Add water, salt, sugar, vegetable bouillon cube, and tamarind water, and stir well. Bring to a boil and let it thicken into a sauce.

7. Add the tofu and potato cubes and mix well.

8. Serve with white rice.

SAYUR DAUN SINGKONG

Cassava leaf sayur

"Sayur" means "vegetables". This almost soup-like Indonesian vegetable dish always consists of one or more types of vegetables, prepared with various spices in a generous amount of coconut milk or broth.

FELIX PONTOH

 MAIN COURSE   VEGETARIAN   SERVES 4   FELIX PONTOH

500 g cassava leaves (daun singkong)
4 tablespoons oil
400 ml coconut milk
salt

BUMBU
5 candlenuts (kemiri nuts)
2 teaspoons ground coriander (ketumbar)
1 teaspoon ground cumin (djinten)
5 shallots, peeled
1 red Spanish chili pepper (lombok)
5 bird's eye chilies (rawit)
3 cm fresh turmeric

1. Grind the ingredients for the bumbu into a paste using a food processor or mortar and pestle.

2. Wash and finely chop the cassava leaves.

3. Heat the oil in a wok and sauté the bumbu until it starts to change color.

4. Add the chopped cassava leaves and mix well. Cook for 2 minutes.

5. Stir in the coconut milk and simmer until the oil floats to the top.

6. Season with salt.

SAYUR KUBIS

Cabbage sayur

■

*Candlenuts resemble hazelnuts.
No matter how appealing they may look, it's better not to eat them raw.
Because they are mildly toxic, they should be cooked or roasted first.*

FELIX PONTOH

 MAIN COURSE   VEGAN   SERVES 4   FELIX PONTOH

1 small white cabbage
1 medium onion
3 garlic cloves
3 candlenuts (kemiri nuts)
2 tablespoons oil
1 to 2 teaspoons sambal oelek
1 teaspoon ground coriander (ketumbar)
1 makrut lime leaf (djeruk purut)
2 tablespoons tamarind water
200 ml coconut milk
salt

1. Cut the cabbage in half and remove the tough outer leaves and the core. Thinly slice the cabbage using a mandoline or sharp knife.

2. Peel and finely chop the onion and garlic. Crush the candlenuts in a mortar and pestle.

3. Heat the oil in a wok and sauté the onion and garlic for 5 minutes, stirring constantly.

4. Add the crushed candlenuts, sambal, and ground coriander and sauté for another 5 minutes, stirring continuously.

5. Then add the cabbage, makrut lime leaf, tamarind water, coconut milk, and salt to taste. Simmer for another 5 minutes until the oil from the coconut milk rises to the surface.

T3 BUMBU BALI

Tofu, tempeh, and telor (egg)

■

The three "t's" of tahu, tempe, and telor (tofu, tempeh, and egg) come together in this dish seasoned with a spice paste from Bali.
VERA ATIKA

 MAIN COURSE   VEGETARIAN   SERVES 4   VERA ATIKA

250 ml oil
180 g tempeh, cut into cubes
150 g tofu, cut into cubes
100 ml water
1½ teaspoons salt
50 g sugar
1 teaspoon ground white pepper
4 hard-boiled eggs, peeled
100 ml sweet soy sauce (kecap manis)

BUMBU
120 g onions, peeled
10 g garlic, peeled
20 g candlenuts (kemiri nuts)
120 g fresh ginger, peeled
50 g red Spanish chili peppers (lombok)
130 g Romano (sweet pointed) peppers, cut into pieces
50 g sambal oelek

1. Heat 150 ml oil in a frying pan and fry the tempeh and tofu until golden brown and crispy. Remove from the pan and set aside.

2. Coarsely chop the ingredients for the bumbu, then grind them into a smooth paste using a food processor or blender.

3. Heat 100 ml oil in a wok and sauté the spice mix over low heat, stirring constantly, for 5 to 6 minutes until it starts to brown.

4. Add the water, salt, sugar, and white pepper. Stir well and simmer gently for 3 minutes.

5. Add the tempeh, tofu, and eggs, and simmer for another 5 minutes.

6. Stir in the sweet soy sauce, mix well, and cook for another 2 minutes.

7. Serve with white rice.

TAHU ACAR

Tofu in sweet-and-sour sauce

■

Many people enjoy sweet-and-sour flavors, and this combination with tofu and white cabbage is truly heavenly.
DONNI SETIAWAN SUGANDA

 MAIN COURSE   VEGAN   SERVES 4   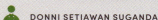 DONNI SETIAWAN SUGANDA

250 g tofu
oil for deep-frying
500 ml water
2 garlic cloves, peeled and finely chopped
50 g palm sugar (gula djawa)
1½ tablespoons sugar
¼ teaspoon ground white pepper
½ teaspoon salt
2 tablespoons sweet soy sauce (kecap manis)
1 tablespoon vinegar
100 g rice noodles, precooked for 2 minutes In boiling water, then rinsed with cold water
50 g white cabbage, sliced
50 g bean sprouts
75 g cucumber, sliced into half moons
25 g peanuts
2 sprigs of celery leaves, chopped
2 tablespoons crispy fried shallots (bawang goreng)

1. Cut the tofu into 2 x 2-cm cubes. Heat a generous amount of oil in a deep pan and fry the tofu cubes until golden brown. Remove them from the pan and drain on paper towels.

2. Bring the water to a boil in a saucepan and add the garlic, palm sugar, sugar, white pepper, salt, sweet soy sauce, and vinegar. Stir and bring back to a boil, then let the broth simmer for 5 minutes.

3. Divide the rice noodles, cabbage, bean sprouts, cucumber, and peanuts over deep plates or bowls and ladle in the hot broth.

4. Garnish with the celery leaves and crispy fried shallots.

TAHU GORENG ASAM MANIS

Fried tofu with tamarind sauce

■

Tamarind gives this dish a delightful tangy flavor.
UMA PHETKAW

 MAIN COURSE   VEGAN   SERVES 4   UMA PHETKAW

500 g tofu
rice oil for deep-frying

SAUCE
80 g palm sugar (gula djawa)
80 ml tamarind water
2 tablespoons light soy sauce
1 teaspoon salt

GARNISH
2 dried chili peppers
15 g cilantro, coarsely chopped
1 to 2 tablespoons white sesame seeds

1. Slice the tofu into 8 pieces.

2. Heat a generous amount of rice oil in a wok and fry the tofu slices until golden brown on both sides, about 5 to 6 minutes. Remove them from the pan, drain on paper towels, and set aside.

3. Remove most of the oil from the wok. Fry the dried chili peppers for the garnish for about 2 minutes in the hot oil until crisp. Remove them from the pan and set aside.

4. Heat the wok and add the sauce ingredients and a splash of water. Bring to a boil while stirring and let it thicken into a sauce for about 1 minute. Remove from the heat.

5. Place the fried tofu slices on a plate and pour the sauce over the slices. Garnish with the crispy fried chili peppers, cilantro, and sesame seeds.

6. Serve with white rice.

TAHU TEMPE TAUCO

Tofu and tempeh in tauco sauce

■

Tofu and tempeh, both made from soybeans, are delicious in this full-flavored tauco sauce. Tauco (taotjo) is a paste made from fermented soybeans and can be purchased in Asian food stores. This dish features three forms of soybeans, showcasing their versatility.

MULFI YASIR

 MAIN COURSE   VEGAN   SERVES 4    MULFI YASIR

6 tablespoons oil
250 g firm tofu, cut into cubes
250 g tempeh, cut into cubes
4 garlic cloves, finely chopped
1 onion, peeled and chopped
5 cm fresh ginger, peeled and finely grated
3 tablespoons vegetarian oyster sauce (optional)
4 tablespoons fermented soybean paste (tauco)
5 makrut lime leaves (djeruk purut)
1 lemongrass (sereh) stalk, bruised
2 tablespoons soy sauce
3 tablespoons sugar
20 g cornstarch
50 ml cold water
1 red bell pepper, cut into strips
1 green Spanish chili pepper, sliced into rings

1. Heat 3 tablespoons of the oil in a wok and stir-fry the tofu and tempeh until brown, about 3 to 5 minutes. Transfer them from the wok to a plate and set aside.

2. Heat the remaining 3 tablespoons of oil in the wok and sauté the garlic, onion, and ginger until golden brown, stirring constantly.

3. Add the vegetarian oyster sauce (if using), fermented soybean paste, makrut lime leaves, lemongrass, soy sauce, and sugar. Stir well, then bring to a boil. Dissolve the cornstarch in the water, add it to the sauce, and let it thicken as it boils.

4. Add the tofu, tempeh, bell pepper, and green chili. Stir, and simmer for another 1 to 2 minutes.

TELUR SEMUR

Eggs stewed in sweet soy sauce

■

In Indonesia, telur semur is a favorite dish, and every family has their own recipe. For me, this dish holds a very specific meaning because I strongly associate it with the riots of May 1998. My mother sheltered Chinese children with us to protect them from the unrest (especially Chinese Indonesians were targeted during this uprising). Towards the end, we ate eggs for a whole week because that's all my mother had to feed us. Telur semur was one of the dishes she made from the eggs.

TIRTA SULAMIT

 MAIN COURSE OR SIDE DISH   VEGETARIAN   SERVES 4 OR 6   TIRTA SULAMIT

2 tablespoons oil
2 onions, peeled and chopped
2 to 3 garlic cloves, finely chopped
1 vegetable bouillon cube
½ tablespoon ground coriander (ketumbar)
pepper and salt to taste
1 liter water
2 boiled eggs, peeled
4 medium potatoes, peeled and cut into cubes
5 tablespoons sweet soy sauce (kecap manis)
50 g dried vermicelli

1. Heat the oil in a wok and sauté the onions and garlic, stirring constantly, until fragrant and golden in color.

2. Add the bouillon cube and ground coriander, and season with pepper and salt to taste. Mix well.

3. Pour in the water, eggs, and potatoes. Stir well.

4. Add the soy sauce and bring to a gentle boil while stirring. Simmer over low heat for 30 to 60 minutes until the potatoes are fully cooked.

5. Taste, and adjust the seasoning if necessary with additional soy sauce, pepper, and salt.

6. Add the vermicelli to the boiling semur and let it soften before serving.

TEMPE SAMBAL MATAH

Fried tempeh with sambal matah

*In Indonesia, we refer to fried food as "gorengan."
In some parts of Indonesia, we pair gorengan dishes with sambal.
Sambal matah can be served with fried tofu, fried tempeh, or—as they do in Manado,
the capital of North Sulawesi where I come from—with fried banana.
Indonesia and sambal: always a good combination.*

TIRTA SULAMIT

 MAIN COURSE OR SIDE DISH   VEGAN   SERVES 4 OR 6   TIRTA SULAMIT

400 g tempeh
200 g self-rising flour
100 g rice flour
½ teaspoon garlic powder
100 ml water
pepper and salt
oil for deep-frying

SAMBAL MATAH
5 bird's eye chilies (rawit)
5 red Spanish chili peppers (lombok)
5 shallots
2 lemongrass (sereh) stalks
4 makrut lime leaves (djeruk purut)
juice of 1 lime
1 to 2 tablespoons oil, plus extra for frying
pinch of salt
1½ teaspoons sugar

1. Slice the tempeh into thin slices.

2. Make a batter using the self-rising flour, rice flour, garlic powder, and some pepper and salt. Dip the slices of tempeh, one at a time, first in water and then in the batter.

3. Heat the oil to 160°C in a pan. Fry the slices of tempeh until they turn golden brown, then remove from the pan and drain on paper towels.

4. Grind all of the ingredients for the sambal into a paste using a food processor or mortar and pestle.

5. Heat a little oil in a pan and sauté the sambal paste until fragrant.

6. Serve the tempeh with the sambal on the side.

TERONG BAKAR PECAK PATI

Grilled eggplant

■

This dish hails from Brebes, located in Central Java. It's one of those signature dishes that people in the countryside prepare using ingredients from their own gardens or those of their neighbors. Grilling is essential to this dish, and provides the distinctive grilled flavor and aroma. In addition to eggplant, my grandma also made this with banana blossoms (now available in cans from the brand Fairtrade Original).

DEWI PETERS

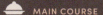 MAIN COURSE   VEGAN   SERVES 4   DEWI PETERS

2 eggplants
4 tablespoons sunflower oil
2 shallots, peeled
2 garlic cloves
3 cm fresh kencur (aromatic ginger)
½ to 1 red Spanish chili pepper (lombok; to taste)
2 Indonesian bay leaves (salam leaves)
4 cm fresh galangal (laos), peeled, halved, and bruised
1 lemongrass (sereh) stalk, bruised
400 ml coconut milk
1 teaspoon sugar
salt

1. Halve the eggplants lengthwise. Sprinkle the cut sides with sunflower oil.

2. Grill the eggplant on the barbecue or in an oven with a broiler (grill) setting at 200°C until the eggplant is halfway cooked, about 15 minutes. Set aside. (If you don't have an oven or a barbecue, you can also use a frying pan.)

3. Finely grind the shallots, garlic, kencur, and red chili using a food processor or blender.

4. Put this mixture in a pan and add the Indonesian bay leaves, galangal, lemongrass, coconut milk, sugar, and a little salt. Stir, and bring to a gentle boil over low heat. Stirring prevents the coconut milk from curdling.

5. Add the eggplant halves and simmer for another 2 minutes.

6. Delicious with rice and tempe goreng.

TERONG KECAP

Eggplant in spiced sweet soy sauce

■

*Eggplant has a deliciously firm texture.
In this delectable dish, it's stewed with spices.*

 MAIN COURSE OR SIDE DISH   VEGAN   SERVES 4 OR 6   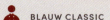 BLAUW CLASSIC

3 tablespoons oil
2 onions, peeled and thinly sliced
2 garlic cloves, thinly sliced
2 eggplants, sliced into half rounds
4 tablespoons sweet soy sauce (kecap manis)
2 Indonesian bay leaves (salam leaves)
150 ml water

BUMBU
4 candlenuts (kemiri nuts)
2 tomatoes, chopped
½ red Spanish chili pepper (lombok), chopped
5 cm fresh ginger, peeled and chopped
1 teaspoon ground cardamom
1 teaspoon grated nutmeg
2 teaspoons ground coriander (ketumbar)
1 teaspoon ground black pepper
½ teaspoon salt

1. Start by making the bumbu. Roast the candlenuts in a dry frying pan and coarsely chop.

2. Grind the chopped candlenuts and the rest of the bumbu ingredients into a smooth paste using a food processor.

3. Heat the oil in a heavy-bottomed pan. Sauté the onion and garlic for 2 minutes.

4. Add the eggplant slices and sauté until they start to brown.

5. Add the bumbu and sauté for another 2 minutes while stirring.

6. Add the sweet soy sauce, Indonesian bay leaves, and water. Stir well and bring to a boil. Stew for 15 minutes until the eggplant is tender.

TERONG MADU

Pan-fried eggplant in a delightful honey sauce

■

A deliciously sticky dish of eggplant in a wonderful honey sauce.
YUNITA DIRMAYANTI

 MAIN COURSE   VEGETARIAN   SERVES 4    YUNITA DIRMAYANTI

2 eggplants, cut into 2 x 2-cm cubes
salt
1 egg
2 to 3 tablespoons flour
3 tablespoons oil
1½ tablespoons honey
1½ tablespoons tomato ketchup
5 tablespoons soy sauce (kecap asin)
1 tablespoon sesame oil
2 tablespoons toasted sesame seeds

1. Place the eggplant cubes in a sieve over a bowl. Sprinkle the cubes generously with salt and let them sit for 15 minutes. Drain off the released liquid and pat the cubes dry.

2. Beat the egg in a large bowl and mix in the eggplant cubes, making sure all of the cubes are well coated with egg.

3. Sprinkle the flour over the eggplant and shake well to coat all of the cubes with flour.

4. Heat the oil in a wok and fry the eggplant cubes until golden brown. Remove the cubes from the pan and set aside.

5. Put the honey, tomato ketchup, soy sauce, and sesame oil in the wok and heat while stirring to make a sauce. Add the eggplant cubes and toss to combine. Garnish with the sesame seeds.

TOFU SAMBAL TAUCO

Tofu in fermented soybean paste

■

Tauco is a dark brown fermented paste made from whole soybeans, wheat, water, and salt. It has a flavor that is sweet, fermented, and dark. Another name for this soybean paste is "taotjo sauce."

YUNITA DIRMAYANTI

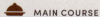 MAIN COURSE VEGAN SERVES 4 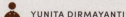 YUNITA DIRMAYANTI

5 tablespoons oil
400 g firm tofu, cut into cubes
1 tablespoon fermented soybean paste (tauco)
2 petai beans (bitter beans)
100 ml water
150 g yard-long beans, ends removed, cut into 3-cm pieces
salt
2 teaspoons sugar

BUMBU
3 banana shallots, peeled and cut into pieces
4 garlic cloves, peeled
3 red Spanish chili peppers, cut into pieces

1. Heat 3 tablespoons of the oil in a wok and stir-fry the tofu cubes, stirring constantly, until they are brown and crispy. Remove the cubes from the pan and set aside.

2. Grind the ingredients for the bumbu into a paste using a food processor or mortar and pestle.

3. Heat the remaining 2 tablespoons of oil in the wok and sauté the bumbu, stirring constantly, until fragrant and golden.

4. Add the fermented soybean paste, tofu, petai beans, yard-long beans, water, a generous pinch of salt, and sugar. Mix well.

5. Simmer gently for 3 to 5 minutes until the yard-long beans are tender.

TUMIS KANGKUNG BAWANG PUTIH

Water spinach with garlic

Kangkung is a delightful vegetable, and extremely popular throughout Southeast Asia.
UMA PHETKAW

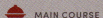 MAIN COURSE   VEGAN   SERVES 4   UMA PHETKAW

500 g water spinach (kangkung)
20 g garlic, peeled
15 g bird's eye chilies (rawit)
2 tablespoons rice oil
15g red Spanish chili peppers (lombok), sliced diagonally
2 teaspoons light soy sauce
1 tablespoon mushroom soy sauce
pinch of salt
2 tablespoons water

1. Trim 3 to 4 cm from the bottom of the water spinach stems. Coarsely chop the water spinach, then wash and allow to drain thoroughly.

2. Crush the garlic and the bird's eye chili into a coarse paste using a mortar and pestle.

3. Heat the rice oil in a wok and sauté the garlic-bird's eye chili paste and the red chili, stirring constantly. Add the water spinach and stir-fry, stirring constantly, for about 3 minutes, until the stems are crisp-tender.

4. Season with soy sauce, mushroom soy sauce, sugar, and a pinch of salt. Add the water and mix well.

5. Serve with white rice

STREET FOOD

JAMUR BUNGKUS KAREE

Mushroom and leek bundles with curry

There's a reason this snack has been on the menu at Blauw for years!

 STREET FOOD   VEGETARIAN   SERVES 4   HENDRA SUBANDRIO

2 tablespoons oil
4 shallots, peeled and finely chopped
6 cm fresh ginger, peeled and finely chopped
4 garlic cloves, peeled and finely chopped
½ tablespoon sambal oelek
1 tablespoon curry masala powder
1 teaspoon turmeric powder (kunyit)
1 teaspoon ground white pepper
1 teaspoon salt
400 g mushrooms, in 1-cm slices
14 spring roll wrappers, 21.5 x 21.5 cm (frozen)
4 pandan leaves
200 g leeks, finely chopped
2 eggs, beaten
oil for deep-frying

1. Heat the 2 tablespoons of oil in a wok and sauté the shallots, ginger, and garlic until the shallots are soft.

2. Add the sambal, curry masala, turmeric, white pepper, and salt. Stir-fry for 1 minute.

3. Add the mushrooms and stir-fry for about 3 minutes. Transfer everything to a bowl and set aside to cool.

4. Thaw the spring roll wrappers. Tear or cut the pandan leaves into 14 long, thin strips.

5. Mix the leeks and eggs into the mushroom mixture.

6. Take a spring roll wrapper and spoon 3 tablespoons of the mushroom mixture into the middle of the wrapper.

7. Fold the wrapper around the filling into a bundle, and tie it closed with a strip of pandan leaf. Continue in the same way until you have made 14 bundles.

8. Heat the oil to 160°C in a deep fryer or wok. Fry a few bundles at a time until they are brown and crispy, about 5 to 6 minutes. Submerge them slightly while frying to ensure even browning.

9. Remove from the pan and drain on paper towels.

KROKET LODEH

Vegetable croquettes

■

Vegetable croquettes with a creamy, spicy filling.
MICHEL E SALEH

 STREET FOOD   VEGETARIAN   8 PIECES    MICHEL E SALEH

FILLING
250 g vegetables, such as finely chopped pointed cabbage, kale, zucchini, carrots, and finely chopped parsley

ROUX
150 g vegan "butter" (such as Violife)
175 g flour
700 ml coconut milk
2 tablespoons vegetable broth
4 garlic cloves, finely chopped
pepper and salt
1 red Spanish chili pepper (lombok), finely chopped (optional)
2 teaspoons agar-agar

BREADING AND FRYING
2 eggs, beaten
50 g flour
150 g panko breadcrumbs
oil for deep-frying

1. Blanch the vegetables you are using for the filling, then drain well.

2. Melt the vegan "butter" in a pan and stir in the flour all at once. Keep stirring until the mixture is smooth. Gradually add the coconut milk, stirring until smooth and thickened.

3. Season with vegetable broth, pepper, salt, garlic, and the red chili (if using). Dissolve the agar-agar in a bowl along with 1 tablespoon of water, then add this to the roux while stirring. Cook for another minute.

4. Mix the drained vegetables into the roux and let the mixture cool.

5. Shape 8 croquettes from this cooled mixture. Let them firm up in the refrigerator.

6. Prepare three plates. Place the beaten eggs in the first, the flour in the second, and the panko in the third.

7. Coat each croquette with flour, then dip in the egg, and finally, coat with the panko; make sure the croquette is completely covered.

8. Heat the oil to 170°C in a pan and fry the croquettes for 6 to 7 minutes until golden brown and crispy.

9. Remove from the pan and drain on paper towels.

LUMPIA TAHU

Spring rolls with tofu

■

*A spring roll is always delicious.
Did you know that the word "lumpia" means "soft pancake"?*

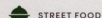 STREET FOOD   VEGAN   16 PIECES   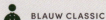 BLAUW CLASSIC

2 tablespoons oil
1 onion, peeled and finely chopped
4 cm fresh ginger, peeled and finely chopped
2 garlic cloves, finely chopped
1 tablespoon sambal oelek
1 teaspoon ground white pepper
1 teaspoon ground coriander (ketumbar)
½ teaspoon salt
200 g tofu, cut into 0.5 x 0.5-cm cubes
100 g carrots, cut into strips
100 g snow peas, trimmed and cut into strips
100 g pointed cabbage, thinly sliced
16 spring roll wrappers, 21.5 x 21.5 cm (frozen)
3 spring onions (scallions), sliced
1 bunch celery leaves, finely chopped
100 g bean sprouts
2 tablespoons sweet soy sauce (kecap manis)
oil for deep-frying

1. Heat the oil in a wok and sauté the onion, ginger, and garlic for 3 minutes, stirring constantly.

2. Add the sambal, white pepper, coriander, and salt; mix well. Add the tofu and stir-fry for 2 minutes.

3. Add the carrots, snow peas, and cabbage, turn up the heat, and stir-fry for 1 minute. Turn off the heat. Put the mixture in a bowl and let it cool.

4. Thaw the spring roll wrappers.

5. Mix the spring onions, celery leaves, and bean sprouts into the sautéed vegetables.

6. Take a spring roll wrapper and spoon on some of the filling. Fold it closed like an envelope on three sides, then roll it up tightly into a spring roll. Brush the edges with water so that the spring roll seals well.

7. Note: Don't make the spring rolls too large; they should be about 10 cm long and 3 cm in diameter. Make sure there are no holes or air pockets so that they don't burst open while frying.

8. Heat the oil for deep-frying in a pan to 160 °C and fry the spring rolls until they are brown and crispy.

9. Remove from the pan and drain on paper towels.

PEPESAN JAMUR

Mushrooms in banana leaves

This snack made from mushrooms is truly delicious.
MULFI YASIR

 STREET FOOD   VEGAN   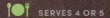 SERVES 4 OR 5   MULFI YASIR

750 g mushrooms
1 tablespoon oil
4 to 5 banana leaves, 20 x 20 cm
50 g leeks, finely chopped
4 to 5 Indonesian bay leaves (salam leaves)

BUMBU
¼ onion, peeled
4 garlic cloves, peeled
3 red Spanish chili peppers (lombok)
2 tablespoons sambal oelek
½ teaspoon ground white pepper
1 red bell pepper, chopped
4 candlenuts (kemiri nuts)
3 cm fresh galangal (laos), peeled and sliced
½ teaspoon ground kencur (aromatic ginger)
4 makrut lime leaves (djeruk purut)

ADDITIONAL EQUIPMENT
aluminum foil
steamer

1. Clean the mushrooms. Heat the oil in a wok and stir-fry the mushrooms over high heat, stirring constantly until they are halfway cooked, about 2 to 3 minutes. Remove them from the pan.

2. Grind all of the ingredients for the bumbu (except for the makrut lime leaves) into a smooth paste using a food processor or mortar and pestle.

3. Mix the bumbu and makrut lime leaves with the fried mushrooms and divide the mushrooms into 4 to 5 portions.

4. Have a steamer ready.

5. Place an unfolded banana leaf on your work surface and spoon on a portion of mushrooms. Sprinkle on some of the leeks and top with a makrut lime leaf. Fold the banana leaf tightly around the filling to form a packet. Then wrap the packet in a sheet of aluminum foil. Make 3 to 4 more packets in the same way.

6. Place the packets in the steamer basket and steam for 15 minutes.

7. Remove the aluminum foil and grill the packets in a grill pan for another 5 to 6 minutes on each side.

PERKEDEL JAGUNG

Corn fritters

■

Delicious snacks that everyone loves.

 STREET FOOD   VEGETARIAN 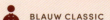 16 PIECES BLAUW CLASSIC

40 g flour

40 g cornstarch

1 egg, beaten

100 ml cold water

1 teaspoon ground coriander (ketumbar)

1 teaspoon ground ginger (djahe)

½ teaspoon turmeric powder (kunyit)

1 teaspoon ground white pepper

1½ teaspoons salt

300 g canned corn kernels, well drained

2 spring onions (scallions), sliced

1 red Spanish chili pepper (lombok), finely chopped

2 garlic cloves, finely chopped

3 sprigs of celery leaves, coarsely chopped

100 ml oil

1. To make the batter, mix the flour and cornstarch in a large bowl. Incorporate the beaten egg and gradually add water until you have a lump-free batter.

2. Stir in the coriander, ginger, turmeric, white pepper, and salt.

3. Add the corn, spring onions, red chili, garlic, and celery leaves to the batter and mix well.

4. Heat the oil in a frying pan. Scoop a heaping tablespoon of batter per corn fritter into the pan. Fry a few at a time.

5. Fry the fritters over medium-high heat until the bottom is golden brown and crispy, then flip and fry the other side. Remove from the pan and drain on paper towels. Continue until all of the batter is used.

PERKEDEL TAHU DONNI

Donni's tofu balls

■

These tofu balls are deliciously crispy.
DONNI SETIAWAN SUGANDA

 STREET FOOD   VEGETARIAN   SERVES 4   DONNI SETIAWAN SUGANDA

300 g tofu
2 spring onions (scallions)
2 sprigs of celery leaves
3 shallots, peeled
1 tablespoon oil
1 egg
½ teaspoon garlic powder
¼ teaspoon ground or grated nutmeg
3 tablespoons flour
1 tablespoon rice flour
1 teaspoon salt
1 teaspoon sugar
1 teaspoon ground white pepper
½ vegetable bouillon cube or ½ tablespoon vegetable bouillon powder
500 ml oil for deep-frying

1. Squeeze out as much moisture as possible from the tofu. Finely mash the tofu with a fork.

2. Finely chop the spring onions, celery leaves, and shallots.

3. Heat the 1 tablespoon of oil in a small pan and sauté the spring onions, celery leaves, and shallots for 2 to 3 minutes, stirring constantly.

4. Combine the tofu with the sautéed spring onion, celery leaf, and shallot mixture and the remaining ingredients (except the oil for deep-frying). Stir well.

5. Form the mixture into balls the size of an unshelled walnut. Flatten them slightly with your hands. Continue until all of the mixture has been used.

6. Heat the oil for deep-frying to 160°C in a deep pan. Fry the tofu balls in the hot oil in batches until golden brown, about 4 to 6 minutes. Turn the balls while frying.

7. Remove from the pan and drain on paper towels.

SATE JAMUR

Mushroom satay

■

You can also make delicious satay with mushrooms.
DONNI SETIAWAN SUGANDA

 STREET FOOD   VEGAN   SERVES 4   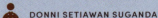 DONNI SETIAWAN SUGANDA

250 g white mushrooms or oyster mushrooms, cleaned
250 ml water

MARINADE
3 garlic cloves, peeled
5 shallots, peeled
4 tablespoons sweet soy sauce (kecap manis)
1 tablespoon sugar
½ teaspoon salt
2 tablespoons oil
½ teaspoon ground coriander (ketumbar)

EXTRA NODIG
5 to 10 wooden or metal skewers
barbecue

1. Bring the water to a boil in a pan, add the mushrooms, and boil for 5 minutes, then drain well.

2. Thread the mushrooms onto the skewers. Place them on a plate or tray.

3. Grind all of the ingredients for the marinade into a smooth paste using a food processor or mortar and pestle.

4. Pour the marinade over the mushroom satay skewers and let them marinate for 5 to 10 minutes. Turn the skewers occasionally to ensure that all of the mushrooms are well coated with the marinade.

5. Grill the satay on the grate of the barbecue until they are brown and cooked through.

SIDE DISHES

ACAR CAMPUR

Mixed pickled vegetables

■

*This is a pickled vegetable dish found in Indonesian,
Indo, and Malaysian cuisine*
MULFI YASIR

 SIDE DISH   VEGAN   SERVES 4   MULFI YASIR

100 g carrots, peeled
100 g white cabbage
1 cucumber
100 g red and green bell peppers
50 g pickled onions, peeled
50 g cauliflower, in small florets

SAUCE
20 cm fresh ginger, peeled
3 garlic cloves, peeled
1 onion, peeled and chopped
750 ml water
7 tablespoons sugar
7 tablespoons vinegar
1 tablespoon turmeric powder (kunyit)
3 tablespoons salt

1. Slice the carrots and cabbage into thin strips; this can be done easily in the food processor or with a sharp knife.

2. Cut the cucumber in half lengthwise. Remove the seeds; this is easy to do using a teaspoon. Cut the halves into thin slices; you can use a mandoline for this if you like.

3. Remove the seeds from the bell peppers and cut them into thin strips.

4. Put the sliced vegetables in a large bowl along with the shallots and cauliflower.

5. Make the sauce. Finely chop or grind the ginger, garlic, and onion; you can use a food processor if you like. Transfer to a pan.

6. Add the water, sugar, vinegar, turmeric, and salt to the pan and heat, stirring until the sugar and salt are dissolved.

7. Let this cool slightly, then pour the sauce over the vegetables. Mix well.

ACAR KETIMUN

Sweet-and-sour pickled cucumber

*Simple and delicious.
A perfect complement to a spicy dish.*

 SIDE DISH   VEGAN   SERVES 4   BLAUW CLASSIC

1 cucumber
2 shallots, peeled
1 red bell pepper
1 teaspoon salt
1 tablespoon sugar
3 tablespoons rice vinegar

1. Cut the cucumber in half lengthwise. Remove the seeds with a teaspoon. Cut the halves into thin slices; you can use a mandoline for this if you like.

2. Cut the shallots into thin half rings. Cut the bell pepper in half lengthwise, remove the seeds, and cut into thin strips.

3. Put the vegetables in a bowl and mix in the salt, sugar, and vinegar. Let this sit for at least 1 hour so the flavors can infuse.

ACAR NANAS

Spicy sweet-and-sour pineapple

■

Fruits can also be a delightful accompaniment to a meal.

 SIDE DISH   VEGAN   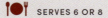 SERVES 6 OR 8   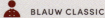 BLAUW CLASSIC

75 g palm sugar (gula djawa), finely chopped
100 ml rice vinegar
2 star anise
4 cloves
1 teaspoon ground white pepper
3 shallots, peeled
1 pineapple
1 red Spanish chili pepper (lombok), finely chopped
1 lime

1. In a saucepan, combine the palm sugar with the rice vinegar, star anise, cloves, and white pepper. Heat until the sugar has melted, stirring occasionally. Let the mixture infuse over low heat for 5 minutes, but don't let it boil. Turn off the heat and let it cool.

2. Slice the shallots into thin half rings. Place them in a large bowl and gently separate the rings with your fingers.

3. Peel the pineapple and cut the flesh into 1 x 1-cm cubes.

4. Add the pineapple to the bowl with shallots and mix in the chopped red chili. Grate the lime zest over the mixture. Pour the vinegar with the spices over the mixture and stir gently to combine.

5. Let the flavors meld in the refrigerator for at least 1 hour before serving.

GOHU

Spicy papaya

∎

*During the four years I spent in Manado, I got used to highly spiced
and spicy food, which was often flavored with bird's eye chili (rawit).
Manado feels like home to me, especially when it comes to delicious food.
This dish of spicy papaya is a fond memory of coming home
and sharing a meal with my family.*

TIRTA SULAMIT

 SIDE DISH   VEGAN   SERVES 4   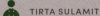 TIRTA SULAMIT

1 papaya, not yet fully ripe
400 ml water

BUMBU
15 bird's eye chilies (rawit)
40 g fresh ginger, peeled
6 onions, peeled
1 teaspoon sugar
2 teaspoons vinegar
salt to taste

1. Peel the papaya and cut the flesh into small cubes. Place in a bowl.

2. Grind the ingredients for the bumbu into a paste using a food processor.

3. Mix the bumbu with the papaya, then add the water and stir well. Chill thoroughly in the refrigerator. It's best served ice cold.

GULAI NANGKA

Spiced jackfruit

■

*Young jackfruit is unripe and green.
Although it doesn't have much flavor of its own,
it absorbs the flavors of herbs and spices exceptionally well.*
PETER DE GROOT

 SIDE DISH   VEGAN   SERVES 4   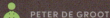 PETER DE GROOT

300 g young jackfruit (nangka), cut into pieces, rinsed
3 g ground white pepper
70 g fresh galangal (laos), peeled and sliced
2 lemongrass (sereh) stalks, bruised, knotted
10 makrut lime leaves (djeruk purut)
30 ml tamarind water
salt, to taste
1½ liters water
400 ml coconut milk
100 g yard-long beans, cut into 6-cm pieces
100 g cabbage, finely sliced

BUMBU
60 g red Spanish chili peppers (lombok), finely chopped
100 g shallots, peeled and chopped
10 g garlic, chopped
30 g fresh ginger, peeled and finely chopped
5 g turmeric powder (kunyit)
20 g ground coriander (ketumbar)

1. Grind the ingredients for the bumbu into a paste using a blender or food processor.

2. Put the jackfruit, bumbu, white pepper, galangal, lemongrass, makrut lime leaves, tamarind water, and salt to taste in a pan.

3. Stir in the water and coconut milk. Bring to a boil over medium heat, stirring regularly.

4. When it boils, reduce the heat and simmer for 1 hour, until the jackfruit is tender. Add hot water if necessary.

5. Add the yard-long beans and cabbage and cook for 20 minutes, until the vegetables are tender.

6. Serve hot with rice. Garnish with a few lemongrass rings, if desired. The cinnamon sticks in the photo are purely for decoration.

NASI GORENG

Fried rice

∎

"Nasi" means "rice," and "goreng" means "fried.
So, "nasi goreng" is "fried rice," and some vegetables,
eggs, and spices are added to this popular dish.

 SIDE DISH   VEGETARIAN   SERVES 4   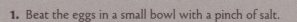 BLAUW CLASSIC

2 eggs
salt
6 tablespoons oil
4 shallots, peeled and finely chopped
2 garlic cloves, finely chopped
1 tablespoon sambal oelek
500 g cooked rice
200 g leeks, very finely chopped
2 tablespoons sweet soy sauce (kecap manis)
1 teaspoon ground white pepper

1. Beat the eggs in a small bowl with a pinch of salt.

2. Heat 5 tablespoons of the oil in a wok or frying pan and sauté the shallot and garlic for 3 minutes. Add the sambal and mix well.

3. Add the cooked rice. Stir-fry the rice over medium heat, stirring constantly, until the grains are light brown.

4. Add the leeks, sweet soy sauce, and white pepper, and stir-fry briefly to mix.

5. Heat the remaining 1 tablespoon of oil in a frying pan and scramble the beaten eggs. Mix the scrambled eggs with the fried rice and season the nasi with salt.

PARE PARE JAWIR

Spiced stewed bitter melon

■

There's a nice story connected to this recipe for pare pare Jawir. I detested the bitter taste of pare (bitter melon)—it reminded me of a drink I was given in Malaysia when I was sick. My mother made the pare drink with the best of intentions, but I found its bitter taste very off-putting and was sure that pare was not for me. That is, until years later, when I went to a restaurant with friends after a yoga class. One of my friends had ordered something that looked green and healthy. I tasted it and loved it. It turned out to be pare pare, and ever since then I've enjoyed it.

PETER DE GROOT

 SIDE DISH   VEGAN   SERVES 4    PETER DE GROOT

450 g bitter melon (pare)
50 ml oil
25 g vegetable bouillon powder
100 g tomatoes, diced
100 g fresh galangal (laos), peeled and sliced
8 Indonesian bay leaves (salam leaves)
150 ml water
salt, to taste
10 g sugar
2 g white pepper

BUMBU
150 g shallots, peeled and chopped
15 g garlic, minced
80 g red Spanish chili peppers (lombok), finely chopped
20 g bird's eye chilies (rawit; optional)

1. Trim the ends off of the bitter melon. Cut in half and remove the seeds. Cut the halves into thin slices, put them in a colander, and sprinkle with a little salt to extract the moisture. Let the slices sit for about 15 minutes. Rinse well, drain, and set aside.

2. Grind the ingredients for the bumbu into a paste using a blender or food processor.

3. Heat the oil in a wok over medium-high heat, add the bumbu and the vegetable bouillon powder, and stir-fry for about 3 minutes, until fragrant.

4. Add the tomatoes, galangal, and Indonesian bay leaves, and stir-fry for another 2 minutes.

5. Add the slices of bitter melon and mix well.

6. Add the water, sugar, white pepper, and salt to taste. Cook for about 10 minutes, until the liquid evaporates and the bitter melon is tender.

7. Transfer to a serving dish and enjoy!

PERKEDEL TAHU YUNITA

Yunita's spiced tofu balls

■

*This is yet another dish that showcases
how everyone puts their own spin on a recipe.
As well as this interpretation by Yunita,
you'll also find Donni's version in this book (see page 143).*

 SIDE DISH VEGETARIAN SERVES 4 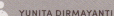 YUNITA DIRMAYANTI

350 g tofu
1 garlic clove, pressed
1 banana shallot, peeled and finely chopped
1 egg, beaten
1 spring onion (scallion), finely chopped
3 tablespoons flour
1 tablespoon white vinegar
ground white pepper and salt
oil for deep-frying

1. Mash the tofu with a fork. Add the remaining ingredients except for the oil. Mix well.

2. Heat the oil to 160°C in a deep pan. Form the tofu mixture into balls using two spoons, then drop them gently into the hot oil. Fry the balls for 4 to 5 minutes until golden brown all over.

3. Remove from the pan and drain on paper towels.

SAMBAL GORENG BUNCIS

Spicy green beans

■

This classic sambal goreng buncis is no longer on the menu at Blauw, but we're bringing it back (and into your home) through this book.

 SIDE DISH   VEGAN   SERVES 4   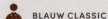 BLAUW CLASSIC

oil for frying
1 onion, peeled and chopped
2 garlic cloves, finely chopped
½ lemongrass (sereh) stalk, cut into pieces and bruised
2 makrut lime leaves (djeruk purut)
500 g green beans
125 g tofu, cut into 1 x 1-cm cubes
salt
½ red Spanish chili pepper (lombok), sliced
100 ml water
25 g creamed coconut (from a block)

BUMBU
4 candlenuts (kemiri nuts)
3 cm fresh ginger, peeled and chopped
3 cm fresh galangal (laos), peeled and chopped
3 makrut lime leaves (djeruk purut), center rib removed
½ red bell pepper, chopped
½ lemongrass (sereh) stalk, just the white part, finely chopped
½ teaspoon salt
1 teaspoon ground white pepper
2 teaspoons sambal oelek
2 tablespoons oil

1. Start by making the bumbu. Roast the candlenuts in a dry skillet and coarsely chop.

2. Grind the candlenuts and the rest of the bumbu ingredients into a smooth paste using a food processor.

3. Heat 2 to 3 tablespoons of the oil for frying in a wok and sauté the onion and garlic for 3 minutes. Add the bumbu, lemongrass, and makrut lime leaves, and stir-fry for 15 minutes, stirring regularly. If it starts to stick, add a little water or oil.

4. Clean the green beans and cut them into 4-cm pieces.

5. Heat 2 more tablespoons of oil in a frying pan and sauté the tofu cubes, stirring, until golden brown. Remove from the pan, drain on paper towels, and sprinkle lightly with salt.

6. Remove the lemongrass and makrut lime leaves from the wok with the fried bumbu. Add the green beans, red chili, and water, then stir and bring to a boil. Simmer for 5 minutes until the beans are al dente.

7. Add the creamed coconut and let it melt.

8. Serve the sambal buncis on a platter, topped with the fried tofu.

SAMBAL TEMPE

Sambal with spiced fried tempeh

There's a reason this tasty, spicy side dish is a classic.

 SIDE DISH   VEGAN   SERVES 4    BLAUW CLASSIC

100 ml oil, plus 2 tablespoons extra

100 g tempeh, cut into 1 x 1-cm cubes

½ onion, peeled and chopped

1 garlic clove, finely chopped

1 tomato, diced

3 red Spanish chili peppers (lombok), sliced

½ teaspoon salt

1. Heat the 100 ml of oil in a frying pan and stir-fry the tempeh cubes until golden brown. Remove them from the pan and set aside.

2. In a mortar and pestle, combine the onion, garlic, tomato, red chilies, salt, and the 2 tablespoons of oil and grind into a paste.

3. Add the fried tempeh cubes and gently crush the cubes, taking care that it doesn't get mushy.

SAUS KACANG

Spicy peanut sauce

■

*This spicy peanut sauce is wonderfully flavorful.
It's also great as a dip for prawn crackers*

 SIDE DISH   VEGAN   SERVES 4   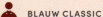 BLAUW CLASSIC

250 g unsalted peanuts, fried in oil
5 tablespoons oil
1 onion, peeled and chopped
2 garlic cloves, finely chopped
1 tablespoon sambal oelek
5 cm fresh galangal (laos), peeled and sliced
5 makrut lime leaves (djeruk purut)
3 Indonesian bay leaves (salam leaves)
2 tablespoons tamarind water
40 g palm sugar (gula djawa)
2 teaspoons salt
juice of ½ lemon
about 150 to 200 ml cold water

1. Finely grind the peanuts in a food processor.

2. Heat the oil in a pan and sauté the onion and garlic for 5 minutes, stirring constantly, until soft.

3. Add the sambal oelek, galangal, makrut lime leaves, Indonesian bay leaves, and tamarind water. Stir, and simmer gently for 5 minutes until it turns into a sauce.

4. Finely chop the palm sugar and add it to the pan along with the salt and lemon juice. Stir, and let the palm sugar melt. Turn off the heat and stir in the ground peanuts.

5. Then turn the heat back on and gradually add the cold water, stirring constantly, until you have a nice, fluid sauce.

SIDE DISHES

SAYUR ACAR KUNING

Pickled vegetables

■

*In Indonesian cuisine, Indonesian bay leaves (salam leaves)
are often used in combination with lemongrass—the two are a truly good match.*
YUNITA DIRMAYANTI

 SIDE DISH   VEGAN   SERVES 4   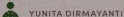 YUNITA DIRMAYANTI

1 cucumber
1 carrot
1 tomato
oil for frying
2 Indonesian bay leaves (salam leaves)
1 lemongrass (sereh) stalk, bruised
2 tablespoons white vinegar
100 ml water
salt
sugar

BUMBU
2 banana shallots, peeled and chopped
3 garlic cloves, peeled
3 candlenuts (kemiri nuts)
½ tablespoon turmeric powder (kunyit)

1. Cut the cucumber in half lengthwise. Remove the seeds with a teaspoon. Cut the halves into strips.

2. Peel the carrot and cut into strips. Quarter the tomato.

3. Grind the ingredients for the bumbu into a smooth paste using a food processor or mortar and pestle.

4. Heat a splash of oil in a pan and add the bumbu, Indonesian bay leaves, and lemongrass. Sauté, stirring constantly, until fragrant and starting to color.

5. Add the carrot, tomato, white vinegar, and water and stir well. Bring to a boil and simmer until the carrot is just tender.

6. Season with salt and sugar to taste, then add the cucumber and mix well. Taste, and adjust the seasoning if necessary.

QUICK NASI KUNING

Yellow rice

■

*Yellow rice with coconut is a colorful
and delicious accompaniment to a rice table.*

 SIDE DISH   VEGAN   SERVES 4    BLAUW CLASSIC

200 g good-quality quick-cooking rice
salt to taste
100 ml coconut milk
50 g creamed coconut (from a block)
3 pandan leaves, knotted
3 makrut lime leaves (djeruk purut)
1 tablespoon turmeric powder (kunyit)

1. Cook the rice in salted water according to the package instructions. Drain when the rice is al dente.

2. Heat the coconut milk over low heat along with the creamed coconut, pandan leaves, makrut lime leaves, and turmeric. Let this infuse for 5 minutes, then turn off the heat. Add the rice and stir well.

3. Cover with a lid and let this sit for 10 minutes.

4. Fluff the rice with a fork before serving.

TELOR KUNING

Eggs in spiced coconut sauce

These deliciously spiced yellow eggs in creamy coconut sauce are made with both coconut milk and creamed coconut.

 SIDE DISH   VEGETARIAN   SERVES 8   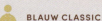 BLAUW CLASSIC

5 tablespoons oil
1 lemongrass (sereh) stalk, cut into pieces and bruised
3 cm fresh galangal (laos), peeled and sliced
2 Indonesian bay leaves (salam leaves)
3 makrut lime leaves (djeruk purut)
100 ml water
8 eggs, hard-boiled and peeled
100 g creamed coconut (from a block)
100 ml coconut milk
150 ml vegetable broth
salt

BUMBU
3 candlenuts (kemiri nuts)
5 cm fresh ginger, peeled and chopped
1 onion, peeled and chopped
2 garlic cloves
1 red Spanish chili pepper (lombok), chopped
5 cm fresh turmeric, chopped
5 makrut lime leaves (djeruk purut), center rib removed, then chopped
½ tablespoon sambal oelek
1 teaspoon salt

1. Start by making the bumbu. Roast the candlenuts in a dry skillet. Put them in a food processor along with the other bumbu ingredients and grind them into a smooth paste.

2. Heat the oil in a wok. Add the bumbu and sauté this for a few minutes, stirring constantly.

3. Add the lemongrass, galangal, Indonesian bay leaves, and makrut lime leaves along with the water. Reduce the heat and let the bumbu mixture simmer gently for 30 minutes, stirring occasionally. Add a little extra water if it gets too dry.

4. Cut the boiled eggs in half and arrange them in an attractive dish.

5. Add the creamed coconut to the bumbu mixture and stir as it melts. Add the coconut milk and vegetable broth and stir until the sauce is nice and thick. Season with salt and pour the sauce over the eggs.

TUMIS BAYAM

Spiced spinach

∎

A quick and flavorful spinach dish.
VERA ATIKA

 SIDE DISH   VEGAN   SERVES 4   VERA ATIKA

3 tablespoons oil
4 garlic cloves, finely chopped
50 g fresh ginger, peeled and finely chopped
1 red Spanish chili pepper (lombok) sliced
200 g spinach
15 ml light soy sauce
½ tablespoon sugar
1 teaspoon salt
1 teaspoon ground white pepper
100 ml water

1. Heat 2 tablespoons of the oil in a wok and sauté the chopped garlic over low heat, stirring constantly, until golden brown. Remove from the pan and drain on paper towels.

2. Add the remaining 1 tablespoon of oil to the wok, toss in the ginger and red chili, and stir-fry for 2 minutes.

3. Add the spinach, soy sauce, sugar, salt, and white pepper and mix well. Add the water and bring to a boil. Allow the spinach to wilt, then immediately turn off the heat. Do not overcook.

4. Transfer the spinach to a beautiful dish and garnish with the fried garlic.

TUMIS JAMUR KEMANGI

Stir-fried mushrooms with basil

Because of their meaty texture, mushrooms are an ideal substitute for meat in a dish.
UMA PHETKAW

 SIDE DISH   VEGAN   SERVES 4   UMA PHETKAW

15 g bird's eye chilies (rawit)
2 garlic cloves, peeled
3 tablespoons rice oil
200 g white mushrooms, sliced
200 g shiitake mushrooms, sliced
150 g king oyster mushrooms, sliced
25 ml water
20 g sugar
½ teaspoon ground white pepper
1 tablespoon light soy sauce
2 tablespoons mushroom soy sauce
5 makrut lime leaves (djeruk purut)
50 g basil leaves

1. Crush the bird's eye chilies and garlic into a coarse bumbu (spice paste) using a mortar and pestle.

2. Heat the rice oil in a wok and sauté the bumbu, stirring constantly.

3. Add all of the mushrooms and stir-fry over high heat for 2 to 3 minutes. Add the water, sugar, white pepper, soy sauce, and mushroom soy sauce. Stir well.

4. Add the makrut lime leaves and basil, then serve.

5. Delicious with rice and cucumber.

TUMIS KANGKUNG

Spiced stir-fried water spinach

■

*Water spinach is not only very tasty but also very healthy.
The leaves contain lots of carotene and potassium.*

VERA ATIKA

 SIDE DISH   VEGAN   SERVES 4 VERA ATIKA

200 g water spinach (kangkung)
5 tablespoons oil
30 g garlic, finely chopped
30 g fresh ginger, peeled and finely chopped
30 g red Spanish chili peppers (lombok), finely chopped
15 ml vegetarian oyster sauce
3 g ground white pepper
salt

1. Wash the water spinach and cut it into 7-cm strips.

2. Heat the oil in a wok, add the garlic, ginger, and red chilies, and stir-fry until the garlic starts to color.

3. Add the water spinach and stir-fry for 1 minute.

4. Season with the vegetarian oyster sauce, white pepper, and a pinch of salt.

SALADS

ASINAN JAKARTA

Fruit and vegetable salad with peanut dressing

■

Who doesn't love mangoes?
Make sure to use a mango that is perfectly ripe.
The mango should still feel firm and not be too soft.
MULFI YASIR

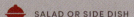 SALAD OR SIDE DISH   VEGAN   SERVES 4   MULFI YASIR

1 mango, peeled and flesh diced
¼ white cabbage, finely sliced
1 green apple, cored and diced
2 cucumbers, diced
50 g bean sprouts (optional)
200 g peanuts, chopped

PEANUT DRESSING
3 tablespoons peanut butter
2 tablespoons sambal oelek
7 tablespoons sugar
2 tablespoons brown vinegar

1. Put the ingredients for the dressing in a large bowl and mix well.

2. Combine the mango, cabbage, apple, cucumber, and bean sprouts (if using) with the dressing. Gently toss to mix.

3. Sprinkle the salad with chopped peanuts.

MIE TERONG DAN SALAD MANGGA

Noodle salad with eggplant and mango

∎

*Rice vermicelli is delicious cold, especially as a salad
with crispy fried eggplant and sweet juicy mango.*
UMA PHETKAW

 SALAD OR SIDE DISH   VEGAN   SERVES 4   UMA PHETKAW

1 eggplant
rice oil for deep-frying
400 g rice vermicelli
50 g basil leaves
50 g cilantro, coarsely chopped
1 mango, peeled and flesh diced

DRESSING
80 ml rice vinegar
45 g sugar
1 teaspoon salt
2 garlic cloves, finely chopped
1 red Spanish chili pepper (lombok), seeds removed and sliced into strips
2 tablespoons sesame oil
zest of 1 lemon
4 tablespoons lemon juice
1 shallot, peeled and finely chopped

1. Put the ingredients for the dressing in a large bowl and mix well until the sugar is dissolved.

2. Cut the eggplant into cubes. Heat a generous amount of rice oil in a wok and fry the eggplant cubes until golden brown. Remove from the pan, sprinkle lightly with salt, and drain on paper towels.

3. Prepare the rice vermicelli according to the package instructions. Drain, rinse with cold water, then drain well.

4. Mix the rice vermicelli with the dressing in the bowl, add half of the basil and cilantro, and gently toss together with the mango cubes.

5. Sprinkle with the remaining basil and cilantro before serving.

PECEL

Vegetable salad with peanut sauce

■

When serving this delicious salad as a main course, you can add a boiled egg or some crispy fried tempeh. Also great with fried emping.

 MAIN COURSE OR SIDE DISH   VEGAN   SERVES 4 OR 8   BLAUW CLASSIC

250 g green beans, ends trimmed
½ cucumber
200 g pointed cabbage
16 radishes
200 g bean sprouts
juice of 1 lime
4 tablespoons crispy fried shallots (bawang goreng)
80 g roasted peanuts, coarsely chopped

SAUCE
3 makrut lime leaves (djeruk purut), center rib removed, then cut into strips
2 bird's eye chilies, chopped
1 onion, peeled and chopped
2 garlic cloves
3 cm fresh galangal (laos), peeled and chopped
1 teaspoon ground kencur (aromatic ginger)
oil for frying
200 g peanut butter
2 tablespoons tamarind water
about 100 to 150 ml cold water
1 tablespoon dark brown sugar
salt

1. Start by making the sauce. Grind the makrut lime leaves, bird's eye chilies, onion, garlic, galangal, and kencur into a bumbu using a food processor or mortar and pestle.

2. Heat a splash of oil in a wok and sauté the bumbu for 5 minutes, stirring regularly. Reduce the heat and add the peanut butter, tamarind water, and sugar. Stir well. Gradually add the cold water until the sauce has the consistency of yogurt. Avoid boiling the sauce to prevent curdling. If it does curdle, remove from the heat and add a little cold water while stirring. Season the sauce with salt and set aside.

3. Cut the green beans in half and cook them in lightly salted water until just tender, about 3 to 5 minutes. Drain, and let them cool.

4. Cut the cucumber into quarters lengthwise, remove the seeds with a teaspoon, and cut the quarters into slices.

5. Slice the pointed cabbage into strips and cut the radishes into wedges.

6. Mix all of the vegetables together and arrange them on a serving platter. Pour the sauce over the vegetables, sprinkle with the lime juice, and garnish with the crispy fried shallots and peanuts.

SALAD MIE JAMUR

Rice vermicelli salad with enoki mushrooms

∎

Enoki or velvet shank mushrooms are fruity and crisp, and ideal for a salad.
UMA PHETKAW

 SIDE DISH   VEGAN   SERVES 4   UMA PHETKAW

500 g rice vermicelli
350 g enoki mushrooms
80 g carrots, peeled and thinly sliced
25 g Chinese celery, cut into 3-cm pieces
100 g small tomatoes, halved
10 g bird's eye chilies (rawit), thinly sliced

DRESSING
30 g sugar
1 tablespoon lime juice
4 teaspoons tamarind water
2 generous tablespoons light soy sauce
1 teaspoon salt
5 g red Spanish chili pepper (lombok), halved, seeds removed and thinly sliced

1. Prepare the rice vermicelli according to the package instructions. Rinse with cold water and drain well. Put the vermicelli in a large bowl.

2. Bring water to a boil in a pan and cook the enoki and carrots for 2 minutes, then rinse with cold water and drain well. Add them to the vermicelli in the bowl.

3. Mix all of the ingredients for the dressing in a small bowl. Add the dressing to the rice vermicelli-enoki-carrot mixture and mix well.

4. Serve with cucumber and white rice. Garnish with the Chinese celery, small tomatoes, and bird's eye chili.

SALAD TAHU JAMUR

Spicy salad with tofu and various kinds of mushrooms

∎

*What's wonderful about this salad is
that it contains three different types of mushrooms.*
UMA PHETKAW

 MAIN COURSE OR SIDE DISH   VEGAN   SERVES 4 OR 6    UMA PHETKAW

---

500 ml water
500 g tofu, cut into four slices
rice oil for frying
200 g oyster mushrooms, torn into pieces
150 g king oyster mushrooms, sliced
150 g shiitake mushrooms, sliced
1 shallot, peeled
10 g mint leaves, shredded
15 g cilantro, coarsely chopped
1 spring onion (scallion), sliced
30 g roasted rice powder*

DRESSING
1 teaspoon chili powder
1 teaspoon ground galangal (laos)
2 tablespoons light soy sauce
15 g sugar
½ teaspoon salt

1. Bring the water to a boil in a pan, add the tofu slices, and cook for 5 minutes. Remove the tofu from the pan and pat the slices dry with paper towels.

2. Heat 2 tablespoons of rice oil in a pan and brown the tofu on both sides.

3. Remove the tofu from the pan and mash it with a fork.

4. Heat another 2 tablespoons of rice oil and sauté the mushrooms in batches until browned. Add extra oil if necessary.

5. Mix all of the ingredients for the dressing in a small bowl.

6. Combine the tofu, mushrooms, shallot, mint, cilantro, spring onion, and roasted rice powder in another bowl. Gently mix in the dressing.

7. Serve with cucumber, fresh vegetables, and white rice.

* To make rice powder: Roast 50 grams uncooked rice in a dry frying pan until golden brown; move the pan regularly to keep the rice from burning. Allow the rice to cool, then grind it into a fine powder using a mortar and pestle.

SWEETS AND DESSERTS

BARONGKO

Banana with coconut milk in banana leaves

■

At every party I attended in Makassar, South Sulawesi, barongko was my favorite snack. When my mother made this for us, it wasn't long before my sister and I had devoured everything. You can probably imagine why once you've tasted barongko for yourself!

TIRTA SULAMIT

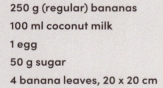

 DESSERT   VEGETARIAN   SERVES 4   TIRTA SULAMIT

250 g (regular) bananas
100 ml coconut milk
1 egg
50 g sugar
4 banana leaves, 20 x 20 cm

ADDITIONAL EQUIPMENT
steamer
wooden cocktail sticks

1. Have a steamer ready.

2. Mash the bananas in a bowl and mix in the coconut milk, egg, and sugar.

3. Wash the leaves and dry them thoroughly. Check to make sure there are no holes in it. Pick up a leaf and use your index finger to press about a third of the way from the top edge and a third from the left edge to fold the corner over, creating a bowl-like shape.

4. Pour a quarter of the banana mixture into the banana leaf and carefully fold it into a packet. Fasten with a cocktail stick. Make a total of 4 packets, then place them in the steamer basket.

5. Steam the packets until cooked through, about 25 minutes.

6. Remove the packets from the steamer, let them cool, then chill thoroughly in the refrigerator.

7. Serve chilled.

BUBUR KACANG HIJAU

Sweet mung bean and coconut porridge

Bubur kacang hijau is often abbreviated as burjo.
It's a sweet porridge made from mung beans, coconut milk, and palm or cane sugar.
Please note that the beans need to be soaked overnight, so start the night before.

YUNITA DIRMAYANTI

 DESSERT   VEGAN   🍽 SERVES 4    YUNITA DIRMAYANTI

150 g mung beans, washed and soaked overnight in plenty of water
600 ml water
1 pandan leaf, knotted
1 cm fresh ginger, peeled and grated
pinch of salt
75 g palm sugar (gula djawa)
65 ml coconut milk
185 ml water

1. Drain the soaked mung beans and put them in a pot with 600 ml of water. Cook them until they are soft.

2. Add the knotted pandan leaf, grated ginger, pinch of salt, and palm sugar to the soft beans. Stir well to ensure that the sugar melts completely and is incorporated into the mixture.

3. Add the coconut milk and water, and bring to a boil while stirring.

4. The porridge is now ready to serve. Garnish with an extra dollop of coconut milk, if desired.

BUBUR KETAN HITAM

Black sticky rice with coconut milk

A delightful, sweet dessert.
HENDRA SUBANDRIO

 DESSERT   VEGAN   SERVES 4   HENDRA SUBANDRIO

150 g black rice
500 ml water
4 pandan leaves, knotted
100 g palm sugar (gula djawa), cut into pieces
100 ml coconut milk

1. Wash the rice and put it in a pot with the water.

2. Add the knotted pandan leaves and bring the rice to a boil. Once the rice is boiling, reduce the heat and simmer gently for 45 minutes. Stir occasionally.

3. After the rice has cooked, remove the pandan leaves and add the palm sugar. Stir well and allow the palm sugar to melt. Let this cool.

4. Spoon the rice pudding into glasses or bowls and drizzle with a splash of coconut milk.

ES CENDOL

Chilled coconut beverage with pandan jellies

■

Delicious and refreshing, this is a beverage you can both drink and eat.

 DESSERT   VEGAN   SERVES 4   BLAUW CLASSIC

100 g palm sugar (gula djawa), cut into pieces
50 ml water
1 can ripe jackfruit (nangka) in syrup, drained
ice cubes
400 ml coconut milk

PANDAN JELLIES
bowl of ice cubes with water
400 ml water
30 g mung bean flour (tepung hun kwe)
1 tablespoon cornstarch
2 tablespoons sugar
1 tablespoon pandan paste
pinch of salt

1. Start with the pandan jellies. Place a colander over a bowl filled with ice cubes and water, making sure that the colander doesn't touch the water.

2. Put 400 ml water in a saucepan and stir in the mung bean flour, cornstarch, sugar, pandan paste, and pinch of salt. Heat, and continue to stir until it cooks into a thick paste. Boil for another 30 seconds, then remove the pan from the heat.

3. Scoop small portions of the hot paste into the sieve and press the paste through the holes, preferably using a silicone spatula. The drops of paste will fall into the ice water and solidify into jellybean-like shapes. Store these in the ice water until needed.

4. In a small pan, combine the palm sugar and 50 ml water. Heat until the sugar melts, creating a syrup. Let this cool.

5. Slice the jackfruit into thin strips.

6. Fill a sturdy plastic bag with ice cubes. Wrap the bag in a kitchen towel and tap the ice cubes with a hammer to create crushed ice.

7. Use four attractive wine or drinking glasses to serve the cendol. Start by putting 3 tablespoons of palm sugar syrup into each glass, or adjust this amount to taste.

8. Spoon some crushed ice onto the syrup, followed by a few spoonfuls of pandan jellies. Pour 100 ml of coconut milk into each glass and garnish with the jackfruit strips.

KUE UBI MANIS

Indonesian sweet potato pancakes

∎

The sweet potato in these little pancakes is a delightful surprise.
DONNI SETIAWAN SUGANDA

 DESSERT   VEGAN   SERVES 4    DONNI SETIAWAN SUGANDA

400 g steamed sweet potato
200 g glutinous rice flour
8 tablespoons sugar
1 teaspoon salt
200 ml water
65 ml coconut milk
oil for greasing the pan

ADDITIONAL EQUIPMENT
Dutch "poffertjes" pan or other pan for tiny pancakes

1. Mash the steamed sweet potato into a smooth, uniform puree.

2. Put the glutinous rice flour, sugar, and salt in a bowl and stir to combine. Gradually add the water and coconut milk while stirring, until the batter is lump-free. Stir in the mashed sweet potato.

3. Heat the pancake pan and lightly grease each cavity with oil. Spoon some of the batter into each cavity. Flip the pancakes when the tops begin to dry, and cook the other side until brown.

PUDING SANTAN PANDAN

Coconut pandan pudding

A delicious pudding made with coconut and pandan.
DONNI SETIAWAN SUGANDA

 DESSERT　　 VEGAN　　 SERVES 4　　 DONNI SETIAWAN SUGANDA

3 packets agar-agar (7 g each)
350 g sugar
1.5 liters water
1 teaspoon pandan paste
1 tablespoon cornstarch, mixed with 2 tablespoons cold water
800 ml thin coconut milk
pinch of salt
1 pandan leaf, knotted

1. In a large saucepan, combine 2 packets of agar-agar, half of the sugar, all of the water, and the pandan paste. Stir together and bring to a boil, then simmer for 1 minute.

2. Pour the mixture into a square container with a capacity of at least 3 liters, or into several small containers. Let this cool and set up at room temperature for about 2 hours.

3. Cut the pudding into cubes and transfer them to a larger container. Note: Proceed to step 4 only after step 3 has been completed.

4. In a saucepan, combine the remaining packet of agar-agar, the remaining half of the sugar, the cornstarch mixed with water, the thin coconut milk, and pinch of salt. Add the knotted pandan leaf and bring to a boil while stirring, then simmer for 2 minutes.

5. Remove the pandan leaf and pour the mixture over the pandan cubes in the container.

6. Let this cool and set up at room temperature for about 2 hours.

TAPE KETAN HITAM WITH VANILLA ICE CREAM

Black sticky rice pudding

Ketan hitam is glutinous rice that still has its blackish-purple hull, giving it a distinctive black color. The rice is sweetened with two types of sugar: brown sugar and palm sugar (gula djawa). It pairs wonderfully with a scoop of vanilla ice cream.

MULFI YASIR

 DESSERT VEGAN SERVES 4 MULFI YASIR

250 g black glutinous rice
1 liter water
1 pandan leaf, knotted
1 cinnamon stick
250 g palm sugar (gula djawa)
5 tablespoons brown sugar
pinch of salt
1 packet dried yeast (7 g)
vanilla ice cream (vegan), for serving
mint leaves

1. Put the rice in a fine sieve and rinse under cold running water. Transfer the rice to a pan, add the water, and allow to soak for 1 hour.

2. After the rice has soaked, add the knotted pandan leaf and cinnamon stick, and bring to a boil while stirring. Reduce the heat and simmer for 45 minutes, stirring occasionally. The rice should have a porridge-like consistency.

3. Remove the pandan leaf and cinnamon stick.

4. Finely chop the palm sugar and add it to the rice along with the brown sugar and pinch of salt. Stir well to dissolve the sugar.

5. Mix the yeast into the rice and allow to ferment overnight at room temperature.

6. Serve the rice in small bowls with a scoop of (vegan) vanilla ice cream on the side. Garnish with a sprig of fresh mint.

WINGKO BABAT

Coconut cake from Babat

∎

*Babat is a district in the Lamongan municipality in East Java.
Many dishes from Indonesia are named after the regions they come from.
Wingko Babat is one such example: "wingko" (coconut cake) hailing from Babat.
This cake holds special memories for me. My father was a trader, and whenever he went to
a neighborhood where wingko Babat was sold, he would always bring some back home.*

DEWI PETERS

 SWEET   VEGETARIAN   SERVES 4   DEWI PETERS

200 g glutinous rice flour
50 g tapioca flour
350 g sugar
200 g grated dried coconut
8 g vanilla sugar
1 teaspoon salt
50 g melted vegan "butter"
   (such as Violife)
700 ml coconut milk
1 egg, beaten
1 egg yolk, beaten with 1 tablespoon
   water
2 tablespoons sesame seeds

ADDITIONAL EQUIPMENT
24 x 24-cm baking pan

1. Line the baking pan with parchment paper and grease the paper with vegan "butter."

2. Preheat the oven to 180°C.

3. Combine all of the ingredients except the egg yolk and sesame seeds in a large bowl, and mix into a batter.

4. Pour the batter into the baking pan.

5. Place the pan in the middle of the oven and bake for 40 minutes.

6. Remove the wingko from the oven, brush the top with the beaten egg yolk, and sprinkle with sesame seeds. Bake for another 10 to 15 minutes or until the cake is golden brown.

7. Allow the wingko to cool on a rack before slicing. Enjoy with jasmine tea.

ACKNOWLEDGMENTS

Culinary Indonesian cuisine is what we at Blauw strive for, one hundred percent. This takes the whole team working together, and everyone contributes to the experience we want to create for our guests. From the head chef to the service staff, from the dishwashers to our suppliers, I want to sincerely thank each and every one of you for your dedication and commitment.

Together with Terra Publishers, we previously created two Dutch-language cookbooks, *Blauw: Authentieke Indonesische gerechten* and *Sambal: 50 gerechten met pit*. For this third book, we wanted something extra, something that would highlight the team spirit at Blauw. And this is why I asked the team to contribute in the form of recipes for this book.

Vera Atika, Yunita Dirmayanti, Peter de Groot, Dewi Peters, Uma Phetkaw, Felix Pontoh, Michel E Saleh, Donni Setiawan Suganda, Tirta Sulamit, Mulfi Yasir, and my chef, Hendra Subandrio, you are invaluable. Without you, this book would not have been possible.

Writer Joke Boon and photographer Simone van den Berg, you have captured the essence of Blauw so well in words and images. I am incredibly proud of the result. My sincere compliments to you both.

In 2022, Blauw received a Michelin Bib Gourmand. This award is truly a crowning achievement for our work, and challenges us even further to pamper our guests with culinary delights, each and every time. A restaurant cannot exist without its guests, and I'd like to extend a huge thank you to all of our guests who have supported us and remained loyal over the past years, even during the challenging times of the pandemic.

Blauw has become famous for its use of authentic herbs, flavors, and colors. We want to share them with you through these recipes so that you can enjoy a little piece of authentic Indonesia not only in our restaurant but also at home.

Selamat makan!

Henk van Hees,
Owner of Restaurant Blauw Amsterdam-Utrecht.

INDEX

INDEX BY RECIPE NAME

INDONESIAN NAMES

Acar campur 148
Acar ketimun 150
Acar nanas 152
Asem pade nangka muda 72
Asinan Jakarta 184
Bami timun jepang 74
Barongko 196
Bihun goreng kampung 76
Bubur kacang hijau 198
Bubur ketan hitam 200
Bubur Manado / Tinutuan 78
Cager telur Madura 80
Es cendol 202
Gohu 154
Gulai boerenkool 84
Gulai nangka 156
Jamur bungkus karee 132
Jamur masak wijen 86
Kroket lodeh 134
Kue ubi manis 204
Kwetieuw sayur 88
Lodeh tempe pete 90
Lumpia tahu 136
Mie terong dan salad mangga 186
Nangka rica rica 92
Nasi goreng 158
Opor tahu tempe 94
Oseng tempe 96
Pare pare Jawir 160
Pecel 188
Pepes tahu Betawi 98
Pepesan jamur 138
Perkedel jagung 140
Perkedel tahu Donni 142
Perkedel tahu Yunita 162
Puding santan pandan 206
Quick nasi kuning 172
Rendang nangka muda 100
Salad mie jamur 190
Salad tahu jamur 192
Sambal goreng buncis 164
Sambal goreng tahu kentang 102
Sambal tempe 166
Sate jamur 144
Saus kacang 168
Sayur acar kuning 170
Sayur asem 62
Sayur daun singkong 104
Sayur kubis 106
Sop jamur 64

Sop labu 66
Sop sayur santan 82
Sop tahu santan 68
T3 bumbu Bali 108
Tahu acar 110
Tahu goreng asam manis 112
Tahu tempe tauco 114
Tape ketan hitam with vanilla ice cream 208
Telor kuning 174
Telur semur 116
Tempe sambal matah 118
Terong bakar pecak pati 120
Terong kecap 122
Terong madu 124
Tofu sambal tauco 126
Tumis Bayam 176
Tumis jamur kemangi 178
Tumis kangkung 180
Tumis kangkung bawang putih 128
Wingko Babat 210

ENGLISH NAMES

Bali spice mix (tofu) 108
Banana with coconut milk
  in banana leaves 196
Black sticky rice pudding 208
Black sticky rice with coconut milk 200
Cabbage sayur 106
Cassava leaf sayur 104
Chilled coconut beverage with pandan
  jellies 202
Coconut cake from Babat 210
Coconut pandan pudding 206
Corn fritters 140
Donni's tofu balls 142
Eggplant in spiced sweet soy sauce 122
Eggs in spiced coconut sauce 174
Eggs stewed in sweet soy sauce 116
Fried eggs in a spicy sauce 80
Fried rice 158
Fried tempeh with sambal matah 118
Fried tofu with tamarind sauce 112
Fruit and vegetable salad
  with peanut dressing 184
Grilled eggplant 120
Indonesian sweet potato pancakes 204
Jackfruit in a spiced sauce 72
Jackfruit in a spicy sauce 92
Mixed pickled vegetables 148
Mushroom and leek bundles with curry 132
Mushroom satay 144

Mushrooms in banana leaves 138
Noodle salad with eggplant
  and mango 186
Noodles made from zucchini 74
Pan-fried eggplant in a delightful
  honey sauce 124
Pickled vegetables 170
Pumpkin soup 66
Rice noodles with vegetables 88
Rice vermicelli salad with enoki
  mushrooms 190
Sambal with spiced fried tempeh 166
Sesame-flavored sautéed mushrooms 86
Soup with tofu, vegetables, and coconut 68
Spiced jackfruit 156
Spiced rice with vegetables 78
Spiced spinach 176
Spiced stewed bitter melon 160
Spiced stir-fried water spinach 180
Spicy fried tofu and potatoes 102
Spicy green beans 164
Spicy kale curry 84
Spicy mushroom broth 64
Spicy papaya 154
Spicy peanut sauce 168
Spicy salad with tofu and various kinds
  of mushrooms 192
Spicy stewed young jackfruit 100
Spicy sweet-and-sour pineapple 152
Spring rolls with tofu 136
Steamed tofu in banana leaves 98
Stir-fried mushrooms with basil 178
Stir-fried tempeh 96
Stir-fried thin rice noodles 76
Sweet-and-sour pickled cucumber 150
Sweet mung bean and coconut
  porridge 198
Tamarind soup 62
Tempeh stewed in coconut milk 90
Tofu and tempeh in a spicy, creamy
  sauce 94
Tofu and tempeh in tauco sauce 114
Tofu in fermented soybean paste 126
Tofu in sweet-and-sour sauce 110
Vegetable coconut curry 82
Vegetable croquettes 134
Vegetable salad with peanut sauce 188
Water spinach with garlic 128
Yellow rice 172
Yunita's spiced tofu balls 162

INDEX BY INGREDIENT

Apple
Asinan Jakarta 184
Banana
Barongko 196
Banana leaf
Barongko 196
Pepes tahu Betawi 98
Pepesan jamur 138
Banana shallot
Gulai boerenkool 84
Perkedel tahu Yunita 162
Sayur acar kuning 170
Tofu sambal tauco 126
Basil
Mie terong dan salad mangga 186
Tumis jamur kemangi 178
Bawang goreng (crispy fried shallots)
Pecel 188
Tahu acar 110
Bean sprouts
Asinan Jakarta 184
Kwetieuw sayur 88
Lumpia tahu 136
Pecel 188
Tahu acar 110
Bell pepper
Acar campur 148
Acar ketimun 150
Asem pade nangka muda 72
Nangka rica rica 92
Pepesan jamur 138
Sambal goreng buncis 164
Sambal goreng tahu kentang 102
Sayur asem 62
T3 bumbu Bali 108
Tahu tempe tauco 114
Bok choy
Kwetieuw sayur 88
Candlenuts (kemiri nuts)
Asem pade nangka muda 72
Cager telur Madura 80
Gulai boerenkool 84
Opor tahu tempe 94
Pepes tahu Betawi 98
Pepesan jamur 138
Rendang nangka muda 100
Sambal goreng buncis 164
Sayur acar kuning 170
Sayur asem 62
Sayur daun singkong 104
Sayur kubis 106

T3 bumbu Bali 108
Telor kuning 174
Terong kecap 122
Cardamom
Rendang nangka muda 100
Terong kecap 122
Carrot
Acar campur 148
Bihun goreng kampung 76
Kroket lodeh 134
Lumpia tahu 136
Salad mie jamur 190
Sayur acar kuning 170
Sop sayur santan 82
Sop tahu santan 68
Cassava
Bubur Manado / Tinutuan 78
Cauliflower
Acar campur 148
Celery
Bihun goreng kampung 76
Lumpia tahu 136
Perkedel jagung 140
Perkedel tahu Donni 142
Tahu acar 110
Chili pepper
Tahu goreng asam manis 112
Chili powder (ground chili pepper)
Salad tahu jamur 192
Chili sauce
Bubur Manado / Tinutuan 78
Chinese celery
Salad mie jamur 190
Chinese kale
Sayur asem 62
Choi sam
Kwetieuw sayur 88
Cilantro
Mie terong dan salad mangga 186
Opor tahu tempe 94
Salad tahu jamur 192
Sop jamur 64
Sop tahu santan 68
Tahu goreng asam manis 112
Cinnamon stick
Rendang nangka muda 100
Tape ketan hitam met with vanilla ice cream 208
Clove
Acar nanas 152

Coconut
Rendang nangka muda 100
Wingko Babat 210
Coconut cream
Sop sayur santan 82
Coconut milk
Barongko 196
Bubur kacang hijau 198
Bubur ketan hitam 200
Es cendol 202
Gulai boerenkool 84
Gulai nangka 156
Kroket lodeh 134
Kue ubi manis 204
Lodeh tempe pete 90
Opor tahu tempe 94
Puding santan pandan 206
Quick nasi kuning 172
Rendang nangka muda 100
Sayur daun singkong 104
Sayur kubis 106
Sop labu 66
Sop tahu santan 68
Telor kuning 174
Terong bakar pecak pati 120
Wingko Babat 210
Corn
Bubur Manado / Tinutuan 78
Perkedel jagung 140
Sayur asem 62
Cucumber
Acar campur 148
Acar ketimun 150
Asinan Jakarta 184
Pecel 188
Sayur acar kuning 170
Tahu acar 110
Daun singkong (cassava leaf)
Sayur daun singkong 104
Djahe (ground ginger)
Perkedel jagung 140
Sop sayur santan 82
Djeruk purut (makrut lime leaf)
Bami timun jepang 74
Cager telur Madura 80
Gulai nangka 156
Nangka rica rica 92
Opor tahu tempe 94
Oseng tempe 96
Pecel 188
Pepes tahu Betawi 98

219

Pepesan jamur 138
Quick nasi kuning 172
Rendang nangka muda 100
Sambal goreng buncis 164
Saus kacang 168
Sayur kubis 106
Sop jamur 64
Sop labu 66
Sop tahu santan 68
Tahu tempe tauco 115
Telor kuning 174
Tempe sambal matah 118
Tumis jamur kemangi 178

Djinten (ground cumin)
Rendang nangka muda 100
Sayur daun singkong 104
Sop sayur santan 82

Egg
Bami timun jepang 74
Barongko 196
Bihun goreng kampung 76
Cager telur Madura 80
Jamur bungkus karee 132
Kroket lodeh 134
Kwetieuw sayur 88
Nasi goreng 158
Pepes tahu Betawi 98
Perkedel jagung 140
Perkedel tahu Donni 142
Perkedel tahu Yunita 162
T3 bumbu Bali 108
Telor kuning 174
Telur semur 116
Terong madu 124
Wingko Babat 210

Eggplant
Mie terong dan salad mangga 186
Terong bakar pecak pati 120
Terong kecap 122
Terong madu 124

Enoki
Salad mie jamur 190

Garlic
Acar campur 148
Asem pade nangka muda 72
Bami timun jepang 74
Bihun goreng kampung 76
Bubur Manado / Tinutuan 78
Cager telur Madura 80
Gulai boerenkool 84
Gulai nangka 156
Jamur bungkus karee 132
Jamur masak wijen 86
Kroket lodeh 134

Kwetieuw sayur 88
Lodeh tempe pete 90
Lumpia tahu 136
Mie terong dan salad mangga 186
Nangka rica rica 92
Nasi goreng 158
Opor tahu tempe 94
Oseng tempe 96
Pare pare Jawir 160
Pecel 188
Pepes tahu Betawi 98
Pepesan jamur 138
Perkedel jagung 140
Perkedel tahu Yunita 162
Rendang nangka muda 100
Sambal goreng buncis 164
Sambal goreng tahu kentang 102
Sambal tempe 166
Sate jamur 144
Saus kacang 168
Sayur acar kuning 170
Sayur asem 62
Sayur kubis 106
Sop labu 66
T3 bumbu Bali 108
Tahu acar 110
Tahu tempe tauco 114
Telor kuning 174
Telur semur 116
Terong bakar pecak pati 120
Terong kecap 122
Tofu sambal tauco 126
Tumis Bayam 176
Tumis jamur kemangi 178
Tumis kangkung 180
Tumis kangkung bawang putih 128

Garlic powder
Perkedel tahu Donni 142
Sop sayur santan 82
Tempe sambal matah 118

Ginger root (fresh)
Acar campur 148
Asem pade nangka muda 72
Bami timun jepang 74
Bubur kacang hijau 198
Cager telur Madura 80
Gohu 154
Gulai nangka 156
Jamur bungkus karee 132
Jamur masak wijen 86
Lumpia tahu 136
Nangka rica rica 92
Opor tahu tempe 94
Rendang nangka muda 100

Sambal goreng buncis 164
Sop labu 66
T3 bumbu Bali 108
Tahu tempe tauco 114
Telor kuning 174
Terong kecap 122
Tumis Bayam 176
Tumis kangkung 180

Green beans
Pecel 188
Sambal goreng buncis 164

Green cabbage
Kroket lodeh 134

Honey
Terong madu 124

Kale
Gulai boerenkool 84

Kangkung (water spinach)
Bubur Manado / Tinutuan 78
Tumis kangkung 180
Tumis kangkung bawang putih 128

Kecap asin
Bami timun jepang 74
Jamur masak wijen 86
Salad mie jamur 190
Salad tahu jamur 192
Sop jamur 64
Tahu goreng asam manis 112
Tahu tempe tauco 114
Telur semur 116
Terong madu 124
Tumis Bayam 176
Tumis jamur kemangi 178
Tumis kangkung bawang putih 128

Kecap manis
Bihun goreng kampung 76
Jamur masak wijen 86
Kwetieuw sayur 88
Lumpia tahu 136
Nasi goreng 158
Oseng tempe 96
Sate jamur 144
T3 bumbu Bali 108
Tahu acar 110
Terong kecap 122

Kemangi (lemon basil)
Nangka rica rica 92
Pepes tahu Betawi 98

Kencur
Pecel 188
Pepesan jamur 138
Terong bakar pecak pati 120

Kerrie masala
Jamur bungkus karee 132

Ketumbar (ground coriander)
Gulai boerenkool 84
Gulai nangka 156
Lumpia tahu 136
Pepes tahu Betawi 98
Perkedel jagung 140
Rendang nangka muda 100
Sate jamur 144
Sayur daun singkong 104
Sayur kubis 106
Sop labu 66
Telur semur 116
Terong kecap 122

King oyster mushrooms
Salad tahu jamur 192
Tumis jamur kemangi 178

Kunyit (turmeric)
Acar campur 148
Asem pade nangka muda 72
Bubur Manado / Tinutuan 78
Cager telur Madura 80
Gulai boerenkool 84
Gulai nangka 156
Jamur bungkus karee 132
Pepes tahu Betawi 98
Perkedel jagung 140
Quick nasi kuning 172
Rendang nangka muda 100
Sayur acar kuning 170
Sayur daun singkong 104
Telor kuning 174

Labu siam (chayote)
Sayur asem 62

Laos (galanga)
Asem pade nangka muda 72
Cager telur Madura 80
Gulai boerenkool 84
Gulai nangka 156
Nangka rica rica 92
Opor tahu tempe 94
Pare pare Jawir 160
Pecel 188
Pepesan jamur 138
Rendang nangka muda 100
Salad tahu jamur 192
Sambal goreng buncis 164
Saus kacang 168
Sop jamur 64
Sop tahu santan 68
Telor kuning 174
Terong bakar pecak pati 120

Leek
Jamur bungkus karee 132
Nasi goreng 158

Pepesan jamur 138

Lemon
Mie terong dan salad mangga 186

Lemon juice
Mie terong dan salad mangga 186
Saus kacang 168
Sop jamur 64
Sop sayur santan 82
Sop tahu santan 68

Lime
Acar nanas 152
Sop labu 66

Lime juice
Pecel 188
Salad mie jamur 190
Tempe sambal matah 118

Lombok (Spanish chili pepper)
Acar nanas 152
Asem pade nangka muda 72
Bami timun jepang 74
Cager telur Madura 80
Gulai boerenkool 84
Gulai nangka 156
Kroket lodeh 134
Kwetieuw sayur 88
Lodeh tempe pete 90
Mie terong dan salad mangga 186
Nangka rica rica 92
Oseng tempe 96
Pare pare Jawir 160
Pepesan jamur 138
Perkedel jagung 140
Rendang nangka muda 100
Salad mie jamur 190
Sambal goreng buncis 164
Sambal tempe 166
Sayur asem 62
Sop labu 66
Sop sayur santan 82
Sop tahu santan 68
T3 bumbu Bali 108
Tahu tempe tauco 114
Telor kuning 174
Tempe sambal matah 118
Terong bakar pecak pati 120
Terong kecap 122
Tumis Bayam 176
Tumis kangkung 180
Tumis kangkung bawang putih 128

Maggi cubes
Sop sayur santan 82

Mango
Asinan Jakarta 184
Mie terong dan salad mangga 186

Mint
Salad tahu jamur 192
Tape ketan hitam with vanilla ice cream 208

Mung beans
Bubur kacang hijau 198

Mushroom soy sauce
Sop tahu santan 68
Tumis jamur kemangi 178
Tumis kangkung bawang putih 128

Mushrooms
Jamur bungkus karee 132
Jamur masak wijen 86
Kwetieuw sayur 88
Pepesan jamur 138
Sate jamur 144
Sop jamur 64
Sop tahu santan 68
Tumis jamur kemangi 178

Nangka (jackfruit)
Asem pade nangka muda 72
Es cendol 202
Gulai nangka 156
Nangka rica rica 92
Rendang nangka muda 100

Nutmeg
Perkedel tahu Donni 142
Rendang nangka muda 100
Terong kecap 122

Onion
Acar campur 148
Asem pade nangka muda 72
Bami timun jepang 74
Bubur Manado / Tinutuan 78
Gohu 154
Lodeh tempe pete 90
Lumpia tahu 136
Nangka rica rica 92
Oseng tempe 96
Pecel 188
Pepesan jamur 138
Rendang nangka muda 100
Sambal goreng buncis 164
Sambal tempe 166
Saus kacang 168
Sayur kubis 106
Sop labu 66
Sop sayur santan 82
T3 bumbu Bali 108
Tahu tempe tauco 114
Telor kuning 174
Telur semur 116
Terong kecap 122

Oyster mushroom
Pepes tahu Betawi 98
Salad tahu jamur 192
Sate jamur 144
Sop jamur 64
Oyster sauce
Kwetieuw sayur 88
Tahu tempe tauco 114
Tumis kangkung 180
Pandan leaf
Bubur kacang hijau 198
Bubur ketan hitam 200
Jamur bungkus karee 132
Puding santan pandan 206
Quick nasi kuning 172
Tape ketan hitam with vanilla ice cream 208
Pandan paste
Es cendol 202
Puding santan pandan 206
Papaya
Gohu 154
Paprika powder
Sop sayur santan 82
Pare (bitter melon)
Pare pare Jawir 160
Parsley
Bami timun jepang 74
Kroket lodeh 134
Peanut
Asinan Jakarta 184
Pecel 188
Saus kacang 168
Sayur asem 62
Tahu acar 110
Peanut butter
Asinan Jakarta 184
Pecel 188
Pearl onions
Acar campur 148
Peas
Sop sayur santan 82
Petai beans (bitter beans)
Lodeh tempe pete 90
Sambal goreng tahu kentang 102
Tofu sambal tauco 126
Potato
Sambal goreng tahu kentang 102
Sop sayur santan 82
Telur semur 116
Pineapple
Acar nanas 152
Pointed cabbage
Bihun goreng kampung 76

Kroket lodeh 134
Kwetieuw sayur 88
Lumpia tahu 136
Pecel 188
Pumpkin
Bubur Manado / Tinutuan 78
Sop labu 66
Radish
Pecel 188
Rawit (bird's eye chili)
Asem pade nangka muda 72
Gohu 154
Nangka rica rica 92
Pare pare Jawir 160
Pecel 188
Pepes tahu Betawi 98
Salad mie jamur 190
Sayur daun singkong 104
Sop jamur 64
Tempe sambal matah 118
Tumis jamur kemangi 178
Tumis kangkung bawang putih 128
Red Spanish chili pepper
Pepes tahu Betawi 98
Sayur daun singkong 104
Tofu sambal tauco 126
Rice powder
Salad tahu jamur 192
Salam leaf (Indonesian bay leaf)
Nangka rica rica 92
Opor tahu tempe 94
Pare pare Jawir 160
Pepesan jamur 138
Rendang nangka muda 100
Saus kacang 168
Sayur acar kuning 170
Sayur asem 62
Telor kuning 174
Terong bakar pecak pati 120
Terong kecap 122
Sambal ulek (sambal oelek)
Asem pade nangka muda 72
Asinan Jakarta 184
Jamur bungkus karee 132
Kwetieuw sayur 88
Lodeh tempe pete 90
Lumpia tahu 136
Nasi goreng 158
Rendang nangka muda 100
Sambal goreng buncis 164
Saus kacang 168
Sayur kubis 106
T3 bumbu Bali 108
Telor kuning 174

Santen (creamed coconut)
Quick nasi kuning 172
Rendang nangka muda 100
Sambal goreng buncis 164
Telor kuning 174
Sereh (lemongrass)
Asem pade nangka muda 72
Bubur Manado / Tinutuan 78
Gulai boerenkool 84
Gulai nangka 156
Nangka rica rica 92
Opor tahu tempe 94
Pepes tahu Betawi 98
Rendang nangka muda 100
Sambal goreng buncis 164
Sayur acar kuning 170
Sop jamur 64
Sop labu 66
Sop tahu santan 68
Tahu tempe tauco 114
Telor kuning 174
Tempe sambal matah 118
Terong bakar pecak pati 120
Sesame seed
Jamur masak wijen 86
Tahu goreng asam manis 112
Terong madu 124
Wingko Babat 210
Shallot
Acar ketimun 150
Acar nanas 152
Cager telur Madura 80
Gulai nangka 156
Jamur bungkus karee 132
Mie terong dan salad mangga 186
Nasi goreng 158
Opor tahu tempe 94
Pare pare Jawir 160
Pepes tahu Betawi 98
Perkedel tahu Donni 142
Salad tahu jamur 192
Sambal goreng tahu kentang 102
Sate jamur 144
Sayur daun singkong 104
Tempe sambal matah 118
Terong bakar pecak pati 120
Shiitakes
Salad tahu jamur 192
Tumis jamur kemangi 178
Snow peas
Lumpia tahu 136
Spinach
Tumis Bayam 176

Spring onion (scallion)
Bami timun jepang **74**
Bihun goreng kampung **76**
Bubur Manado / Tinutuan **78**
Jamur masak wijen **86**
Kwetieuw sayur **88**
Lodeh tempe pete **90**
Lumpia tahu **136**
Pepes tahu Betawi **98**
Perkedel jagung **140**
Perkedel tahu Donni **142**
Perkedel tahu Yunita **162**
Salad tahu jamur **192**
Sop jamur **64**

Spring roll wrappers
Jamur bungkus karee **132**
Lumpia tahu **136**

Star anise
Acar nanas **152**
Rendang nangka muda **100**

Sweet potato
Kue ubi manis **204**

Tahu (tofu)
Bubur Manado / Tinutuan **78**
Lumpia tahu **136**
Opor tahu tempe **94**
Pepes tahu Betawi **98**
Perkedel tahu Donni **142**
Perkedel tahu Yunita **162**
Salad tahu jamur **192**
Sambal goreng buncis **164**
Sambal goreng tahu kentang **102**
Sop tahu santan **68**
T3 bumbu Bali **108**
Tahu acar **110**
Tahu goreng asam manis **112**
Tahu tempe tauco **114**
Tofu sambal tauco **126**

Tamarind
Gulai nangka **156**
Sayur asem **62**
Sop jamur **64**

Tamarind water
Asem pade nangka muda **72**
Pecel **188**
Salad mie jamur **190**
Sambal goreng tahu kentang **102**
Saus kacang **168**
Sop tahu santan **68**
Sayur kubis **106**

Tauco (fermented soybean paste)
Tahu tempe tauco **114**
Tofu sambal tauco **126**

Tempe (tempeh)
Lodeh tempe pete **90**
Opor tahu tempe **94**
Oseng tempe **96**
Sambal tempe **166**
T3 bumbu Bali **108**
Tahu tempe tauco **114**
Tempe sambal matah **118**

Thai basil
Bubur Manado / Tinutuan **78**

Tomato
Lodeh tempe pete **90**
Nangka rica rica **92**
Oseng tempe **96**
Pare pare Jawir **160**
Pepes tahu Betawi **98**
Salad mie jamur **190**
Sambal goreng tahu kentang **102**
Sambal tempe **166**
Sayur acar kuning **170**
Sop jamur **64**
Sop sayur santan **82**
Sop tahu santan **68**
Terong kecap **122**

Tomato ketchup
Terong madu **124**

Tomato paste
Sop sayur santan **82**

Vanilla ice cream
Tape ketan hitam with vanilla ice cream **208**

Vegetable broth
Bami timun jepang **74**
Kroket lodeh **134**
Sop labu **66**
Telor kuning **174**

Vegetable bouillon cube
Perkedel tahu Donni **142**
Sambal goreng tahu kentang **102**
Sop jamur **64**
Sop tahu santan **68**
Telur semur **116**

Vegetable bouillon powder
Cager telur Madura **80**
Lodeh tempe pete **90**
Opor tahu tempe **94**
Pare pare Jawir **160**
Pepes tahu Betawi **98**
Perkedel tahu Donni **142**
Sambal goreng tahu kentang **102**

Vermicelli
Telur semur **116**

White cabbage
Acar campur **148**

Asinan Jakarta 184
Cager telur Madura **80**
Sayur asem **62**
Sayur kubis **106**
Tahu acar **110**

Yard-long bean
Sayur asem **62**
Tofu sambal tauco **126**

Zucchini
Bami timun jepang **74**
Kroket lodeh **134**

CREDITS

© 2024 Uitgeverij TERRA
Uitgeverij Terra is part of TerraLannoo bv
P.O. Box 23202
1100 DS Amsterdam
the Netherlands

info@terralannoo.nl
www.terra-publishing.com

 terrapublishing
 terrapublishing

Text: Joke Boon in collaboration with Restaurant Blauw
Photography: Simone van den Berg
Design cover and interior: The Creative Rebels, Sabrina Raams

First print, 2024

ISBN 978 90 8989 989 7
NUR 442

This book uses paper that is certain to have not caused forest destruction. Terra believes it is important to use natural resources in an environmentally friendly and responsible manner.

All rights reserved. No part of this publication may be reproduced, stored in a retrieval system, or transmitted in any form or by any means, electronic, mechanical, photocopying, recording, or otherwise, without the prior written permission of the publisher.